# SCHOOL OF SQUEEZE

# SCHOOL OF SQUEEZE

*Threatened to Thriving in Agribusiness*

## DAN TRACY

Published by Fifth Estate Media

Printed by Ingram Group of the United States of America

Historical photographs contributed by the Brown and Peters families. Photography by Judy Tracy.

Cover illustration by Jesse Kunerth
Graphic illustrations, maps by Jill Shaarga, Shargaa Illustration & Design

Editing by Fifth Estate Media. Proofing by Laureen Crowley

*For our families*

# CONTENTS

# FOREWORD

BY FORMER FLORIDA LIEUTENANT GOVERNOR
AND SENATE PRESIDENT TONI JENNINGS

I've known the Brown family for decades, having been neighbors off and on with them in two different Orlando neighborhoods. The late patriarchs of our two families, Jack Jennings and Jerry Brown Sr., were friends, running in the same social circles, though they did not do business together.

I was fortunate to attend many of the annual Thanksgiving morning Bloody Mary parties thrown by Jerry and his lovely wife Carolyn. Luckily, I was never asked to cook any turkeys post party.

Given my history with the Brown family, what I found most surprising about this book is the many things I simply did not know about them, especially the diligence, perseverance and inventiveness first of the father, then of the sons, Jerry, Jr., (Gator) and Tom, when they took over Florida Food Products.

I knew FFP was successful at processing citrus and owning and maintaining acres of groves, but I never realized that

Brown Sr., was the first person to come up with a way to actually can Coca-Cola, which previously was sold only in the bottle. I also was taken aback by the heroic nature of Brown's experiences during World War II.

Like many of his generation, Brown left the war behind him when he returned stateside. He had to be prodded to talk about the horrors he experienced.

And when Gator and Tom took over the plant in Eustis, they moved away from citrus, realizing all those trees that once were so important to the Central Florida economy now were being uprooted for countless tracts of new houses. The brothers focused their efforts instead on monetizing a variety of under-utilized crops, ranging from sour watermelons and carrots that flunked cosmetic tests to celery powder and aloe.

A college professor could easily use the exploits of the Browns to teach a business class on turning liabilities into assets.

As I got deeper into the book, I could not help but see parallels between my company, Jack Jennings & Sons Construction Services, and Florida Food Products. Both were family owned and operated in greater Orlando, founded by a larger-than-life veteran who handed over his life's work to the next generation.

Both companies were taken to new heights by a pair of sons — Jeff and John for Jennings and Jerry (Gator) and Tom for Florida Food Products. Despite the ups and downs of the national and Central Florida economies, Jack Jennings & Sons and FFP not only survived the challenges, but thrived.

Were they alive today, I doubt that Jerry Brown Sr., or my

father would recognize the operations that were reimagined and transformed by their progeny.

Although Jack Jennings & Sons remains in family hands, Florida Food Products was sold to a venture capital firm in 2016, freeing Gator and Tom to pursue new investment opportunities and adventures.

And after reading this book, I can tell you they deserve any good fortune that comes their way.

*Toni Jennings, a part owner of Jack Jennings & Sons, served twenty four years in the Florida Legislature, eventually rising to Senate President from 1996-2000. She was Lieutenant Governor under Jeb Bush from 2003-07. That earned her the distinction of being the only person in Florida history to be both Senate President and Lieutenant Governor.*

# INTRODUCTION

My life intersected with Tom and Gator Brown in a fairly common way. My wife and Gator's wife were once roommates, so we got to know each other through our spouses. I met Tom through Gator.

Early on, I was introduced to their remarkable parents, Jerry and Caroline Brown. I had interviewed Jerry Brown for a story once during the mid 1980s, but I was too busy with a young family and work to really get to know him or his wife.

Writing a book about their family history dawned on all of us rather slowly. Two things sparked the notion from my side.

1. The multimillion dollar sale in 2016 of the family business that Jerry Brown started in 1954, ending an arduous two-year process for the brothers that I had followed from afar.

2. Family stories Gator shared with me on several hikes we took during vacations with our families, along with several others, took together. In particular, I was enthralled by the stories about Jerry Brown's World War II exploits.

At the end of a holiday party in 2016, I told Gator he and Tom should think about a book, if for no other reason than to let their offspring and future generations of their families know what preceded them. Turns out that others had been encouraging Gator and Tom to do just that.

After some back and forth, we decided to go for it. Countless interviews, lots of research, writing and rewriting later, here we are.

I knew the decision we reached was correct when I was sorting through some Brown records and memorabilia and found a long-ago typed note from Caroline. In it, she suggested that someone should commit the Brown/Peters saga to paper and now, of course, a digital format.

"Maybe someday," she wrote, "our family will do a really good job of putting all this together and saving it."

*Dan Tracy*

# PROLOGUE

The furies of Hell seemed to be raining down on Jerry Brown as he bobbed in the deadly cold of the English Channel. His ship, the LST 507, was in flames and sinking. Pools of oil were burning on the water's surface, producing an evil, reddish glow. An acrid haze was forming in the night air as munitions exploded and guns were fired. Dying and scared men screamed in pain and panic. Help! They cried. I can't swim!

Brown, a newly minted ensign from a small, rural town in Central Florida, had given his life jacket to another man, one who couldn't even tread water and had been hurt when a German torpedo smashed into the midsection of the 507. The ship, which held close to five hundred soldiers and sailors and tons of military equipment, was immediately disabled and doomed, losing all power and electricity.

As an artillery officer on the deck, Brown tried to maintain his calm, just like the captain of the ship, Jim Swarts, who also had surrendered his life preserver to another. In true Navy tradition, Swarts was the last man off, jumping into the frigid water from the sinking stern soon after Brown, who was known to his mates as Brownie.

Would the early morning hours of April 28, 1944, be their last bits of time on Earth?

That was the sad reality for almost six hundred and forty men who died during the World War II training maneuver known as Exercise Tiger. Their ships were attacked by four German E-boats patrolling the Channel. Brown was one of the lucky ones. He made it. His captain, Swarts, did not.

Brown alternately swam and paddled a raft for hours in forty-two-degree water while men froze to death around him, floating face down, buoyed by their ill-fitting life vests. Their cries for help slowly died out as they lapsed into fatal sleeps.

In surviving, Brown became a different man: One who had seen and escaped death, had lost good friends to the horrors of war. And, like many veterans, he would be reluctant to discuss what he lived through during those awful hours and days. Yet those circumstances helped mold him into a man who would not be afraid to take a chance on life or a risky business venture until the day he, too, would die.

Jerry Brown is key to understanding the story of the family he was born into and, eventually, enlarged after marrying his high school sweetheart. He founded a company, Florida Food Products (FFP) of Eustis, that would support him and future generations of Browns.

The Brown saga, in many ways, mirrors the history of Florida, the state they have called home since the late 1880s.

Spawned in the damp heat before air conditioning and tethered to the boom and bust cycle of agriculture, specifically oranges, the Browns slowly, often haltingly, built their enterprise. During the course of a century, they expanded beyond, then abandoned, citrus for more lucrative ventures, much like the rest of the state.

Though the Browns followed a preponderance of the citrus industry in selling off groves and watching them turn into housing developments, they continually retooled their Eustis processing plant. They used the complex to fuel their drive to become an innovative, scientifically complicated and diversified international concern selling numerous food components to buyers large and small. They thrived at following the ancient business platitude of turning liabilities into assets. In short, they squeezed profits from the rejects of others, almost like getting the final drop from an orange.

Eventually, one of their creations, a celery-based powder, became an essential element in the burgeoning billion-dollar-plus, natural processed meat market. That set the stage for their biggest deal: Selling the company and plant in 2016 for a small fortune to a private equity firm from Dallas. Per the sales agreement, the price was not publicly disclosed.

Four generations of Browns have experienced grand successes and deflating failures, continual metamorphoses and miscalculations, multimillion-dollar sell-offs and purchases, scrambles to meet payroll and layoffs. More than once, they faced the very real possibility of losing it all and going broke. Put simply, the Browns and their business have followed a path similar to that of the relentlessly growing metro area of

Central Florida, which they have called home since late in the
Nineteenth Century.

## CITRUS REPLACED BY TOURISM, DEVELOPMENT

Thanks to the advent of air conditioning and a relatively
benign subtropical climate, the region has jettisoned growing
crops in favor of tourism, massive theme parks, almost unfet-
tered commercial and residential developments and a belated
push for high-tech alternatives. All the while, major companies, big egos and small-time schemers have come and gone as
the economy roared and alternately faded.

The Peterses branch of the Brown clan moved from Illinois
around 1888 and made a homestead claim to ninety acres of
sandy soil near the banks of Black Lake in west Orange
County, a few clicks from the small crossroads citrus town of
Winter Garden.

The Peters planted orange trees by seed and built a white,
two-story frame house with green shutters and long sleeping
porches upstairs, the structure drenched in the pungent scent
of the virgin pines they cleared from the property and used for
the walls, floors and studs. Tethered to agriculture, the Peters
thrived when the weather was good. But they suffered through
the freezes that turned pulp inside the oranges to ice, making
them worthless and unsalable as a fresh commodity. If temperatures fell into the twenties and stayed there for hours, the sap
could freeze, killing the trees, too.

Phil C. Peters, whose father moved the family to Black
Lake, Florida, would become one of the most powerful

members of the Florida citrus industry as the long-serving general manager of a Winter Garden Growers Cooperative.

The Browns would settle down a few decades later in Winter Garden after family members moved south twice, first from Calhoun, Georgia, then to North Florida, where they lived in communities such as Fort White, High Springs and Cow Creek in Alachua and Columbia counties, according to the research service Ancestry.

Alexander Z Brown, a fertilizer salesman, and his wife, the former Josephine McCombs, bought a modest frame home on Highlands Avenue in downtown, little more than a block behind what is now the police headquarters. In a quirk no one can really explain, there was no period after the Z in Brown's name.

The Browns had a daughter, Tex, and a son, also named Alexander Z, but who went by the nickname Jerry, after a popular comic strip called Jerry On The Job. In 1934, the father died of a heart attack while driving his car to the hospital after feeling ill. He was fifty-four years old. The children were ages sixteen and twelve, respectively, forcing the widow Josephine to go to work as a secretary to make their tenuous ends meet.

The Peterses were much higher up in the economic strata than the Browns thanks to their reach in citrus, arguably the biggest and most profitable business in the state at that time. Like many in Florida, both the Peterses and the Browns hired African Americans for a variety of chores, from tending their groves and cooking their food to washing their clothes and helping raise their children.

The families paid a fair wage and treated their black workers with respect, abhorring and forbidding any verbal or physical abuse on their watch. The Peterses also built separate quarters for the help on the Black Lake property. As electricity, air conditioning and running water made its way to Central Florida, both the Peters and Browns provided separate bathrooms for those performing domestic chores.

Two black men, Arthur Faircloth and Willie Sager, would spend their entire adult lives working for the Peters and Brown families. A black housekeeper, Barbara Lampkin, would be at the bedside of Caroline Peters Brown when she died.

The families merged when Jerry Brown married the former Caroline Peters on April 2, 1949, during an evening ceremony at the First Methodist Church in Winter Garden. She was the younger, by sixteen months, of the two Peters girls. Her older sister Frances, who went by the name Freck because of her numerous freckles, had become a war-time bride after only a few dates, marrying an Air Force pilot who had been stationed in Orlando. Her husband, Tom McGehee, went on to become a three-star general.

Though the young couple had dated during high school and exchanged letters during World War II, they did not become romantically serious until after he returned home from the South Pacific in February of 1946 — at least that is the way Caroline Peters recalled it. Jerry Brown was fond of telling anyone who would listen that he knew he would marry Caroline the day he first set eyes on her in high school.

But the war and higher education got in the way for both of them.

Brown enlisted in the Navy and became a gunnery officer after working his way through the University of Florida in three years by washing dishes and waiting on tables at student dining halls. He was on a mine-sweeping ship churning for Japan when President Harry S. Truman ordered nuclear bombs dropped on Hiroshima and Nagasaki, effectively ending the war.

Caroline Peters worked in marketing at one of downtown Orlando's finest department stores, Dickson & Ives, after graduating with a psychology degree from Hollins College, an all-women's school in Roanoke, Virginia.

Her union with Jerry Brown led to five children: SuSu Gordy, Brenda Holson, Jerry Jr., Bill and Tom. Their progeny would have come as remarkable news to the doctor who examined Brown after he was plucked from the English Channel following the botched military operation of Exercise Tiger. The physician told the young sailor that he had survived his ordeal in fine shape, but probably would not be able to have children because of the numbing effect of the cold water on his testicles.

## LOAN HELPS SEAL PLANT PURCHASE

FFP was created in 1954 by Jerry Brown and two partners. The trio bought the plant from a company called Golden Gift; the purchase price was lost over time. Brown had worked several jobs after leaving the military, but had always wanted to be his own boss. His first step on his own was the purchase of a packing plant in the small town of Bartow in Polk County, an acquisition he later would sell at a profit. His father-in-law loaned him $10,000 to close the original deal.

Two of Brownie's unexpected children, Jerry, Jr., who answers to the nickname Gator, and Tom, went to work for Florida Food Products during the early- to mid-1980s, each after spending up to two years traveling the world after completing college. Five years apart, they had been given round-trip tickets to Europe as graduation gifts from their father.

The business, when Gator first joined, was failing. His father was in his late 50s and tiring, having recovered from a heart attack a few years earlier. FFP, as a result, had gone from a thriving venture with a high of nearly four hundred employees and plants all over the Eastern Seaboard, plus Puerto Rico, to the nadir of just the Eustis operation and six full-time workers.

FFP had pioneered, during the late 1950s, the canning and filling of carbonated beverages, including Coca-Cola and a variety of private labels, among them Shasta and Fresca. At one point, FFP was the largest contract canner of carbonated beverages east of the Mississippi River. But it was felled by a new set of machinery that did not seal the lids tightly. The result was warehouses filled with canned colas and specialty drinks springing leaks, leading to massive recalls during the late 1960s and the near ruination of the company.

FFP limped through the hyper inflation of the 1970s, retreating back to being a seasonal processor of citrus juice and renting out a hundred thousand square feet of dry and frozen warehouse space in Eustis. A chance phone call from a business associate during the mid 1980s changed the direction of the company almost overnight.

"Can you process aloe?" was the question. Gator, who took the call, answered yes, though he wasn't sure if the company could deliver. In truth, he knew next to nothing about aloe, just like his father. But they figured out a process to make aloe an ingredient in lotions and for drinks and began slowly rebuilding the company.

A second-hand evaporator purchased by Brown Sr., in 1954 was a key component in the company's budding comeback because it boiled off water at low temperatures, which was perfect for concentrating het-sensitive aloe.

Along the way, the company moved into concentrating several different vegetable juices, including carrots they picked up and processed from the incredibly fertile and ooze-filled fields along the north shore of Lake Apopka. The state put an end to what became a lucrative product line by spending nearly two hundred million dollars buying almost twenty thousand acres of muck farms during the late 1990s and restoring the land to its natural wetland state. Fertilizer and pesticide runoff from the fields had polluted and largely killed the lake, leading to some alligators growing up with both sets of sexual organs.

Through the din of long hours, perseverance, risk taking, networking, innovating, tough sales negotiating, overcoming employee theft and some luck, the brothers took Florida Food Products to levels their father might have envisioned, but never quite managed. Brown Sr., died of congestive heart failure in 1995. He was seventy three. His wife passed away in 2007 at the age of eighty six, a victim of brain cancer.

The following pages memorialize the life and times of the

Browns and Peterses. The story is based on dozens of interviews with family members, friends, business associates, agricultural experts, academicians, military records, newspaper articles, company literature, internal financial documents, the Exercise Tiger website, a memoir written by Caroline Peters Brown in 2004 called *Orange Blossom Petals* and a book entitled *Exercise Tiger* by Nigel Lewis published in 1990.

On April 28, 2018, the Brown family commemorated the seventy-fourth anniversary of the Exercise Tiger tragedy at the Slapton Ley National Nature Reserve, which is on the southwest coast of Great Britain. Standing (left to right) on the front row: Lisa Brown, Brenda Holson, and SuSu Gordy. Back row: Jerry "Gator" Brown, Yates Rumbley, Tom Brown, Bruce Gordy.

# I

## THE SALE

### END GAME FOR DECADES OF REINVENTION

Hurricane Matthew was roiling the Atlantic waters off the East Coast of Florida. Once a deadly Category Five, Matthew still possessed winds of more than one hundred and ten miles per hour after it had battered Haiti, Cuba and the northern Bahamas. No one could say for sure if it would come ashore in Florida or stay out to sea. As the owners of Florida Food Products (FFP) in Eustis, Jerry and Tom Brown decided to close the plant fifty miles inland in rural Lake County and allow their eighty-some employees to weather the storm at their homes.

The date was October 7, 2016 and rain propelled sideways by fifty-mph winds was pelting the state during the dark morning hours. It was an unforgettable time for the Brown brothers for more reasons than just Matthew, the outer bands of which were pummeling the walls and windows of the company compound their late father had founded with two partners in 1954 – one year before Jerry was born.

The morning of October 7, 2016 also was the day that they were finalizing the sale of FFP to Kainos Capital, a Dallas private equity firm. The price was not publicly disclosed, but it was a multi-million dollar deal, plus a percentage of the proceeds when Kainos resold FFP. The second sale — again at an undisclosed price — was to another private equity firm during the summer of 2018. The brothers also arranged for three million dollars to be split among a dozen long-serving employees when Kainos finalized the subsequent sale.

Jerry Brown Jr., who is named after his father but goes by his childhood moniker of Gator, was in his office at the nearly deserted complex. The company comptroller — Wendy Richards — was the only other person on-site. Tom Brown, the younger brother by five years, was at his Winter Park home with one of his two daughters, Taylor, then a student at Rollins College.

Both sons resemble their father, Alexander Z "Jerry" Brown Sr., in their looks and approach to life. They are stocky, balding, their eyes blue. They smile easily, exhibit strong Southern manners — Yes, ma'am, No, sir — and their humor often is self deprecating. They are not afraid to laugh at themselves and are reluctant to poke fun at others. Like their father, their knowledge of FFP and the food-ingredients industry in which they operated is encyclopedic. Registered Republicans, they lean right politically and financially, but drift a bit to the left socially. Like many voters, they do not fit neatly into one camp or the other. Much like their patriarch, they aren't afraid to take a risk and live with the consequences, good or bad.

Brown Sr., who died of congestive heart failure in 1995, was very much on their minds as they dialed into a conference call with nearly a dozen Kainos officials and assorted number crunchers. It was bottom-line time – yea or nay on the deal. The call was largely perfunctory, but last-minute details had cropped up before to derail business arrangements they had made in the past, though none was ever as big or momentous as this one. Would everyone finally sign off, ending what had become a gut-wrenching process that had consumed two years of their lives?

Gator was keyed up, ready for the proposed sale to go through. He wanted it done, to move on to whatever the future had in store for him. Tom was more equable. He displayed no anxiousness. He would live with the call one way or the other.

Their divergent reactions were in line with their personalities. Gator is sentimental, easily cries in joy and sorrow, and is a bit reticent to voice an opinion, occasionally overthinking a problem. At FFP, he was the inside man, the guy who ran the plant, keeping everything on schedule. Tom is more stoic, quicker to act. He was the outside guy, the one who went on the road up to six weeks at a stretch, making cold calls, selling FFP to customers large and small around the world. He also handled marketing, research and regulatory concerns. Sometimes the two disagreed on how to move forward, but eventually they would compromise or come around to the other's point of view.

"They could be critical of each other," said John Simmons, a Tampa executive who was hired by the brothers to help engineer the sale. "But their love for each other and family is more important than business."

Like Brown Sr., Gator and Tom gave their all to FFP, shepherding the company through good times and bad. Working long hours, often including nights and weekends, they orchestrated transformations in product lines, production capabilities and delivery systems, reinventing the company time and again. They became experts at the art of squeezing, as in getting the last drop out every venture they undertook, from oranges to cabbage-based hair dye to the celery powder they modified based on the expertise of a University of Florida adjunct professor who would revolutionize the natural processed meat market.

An aerial of Florida Food Products shows the evaporators to the middle left.

The brothers became owners of the plant during the early 1990s, when Brown Sr., perhaps sensing his mortality, decided to divvy up his holdings among his five children. Gator and Tom were given 25 percent of the stock in FFP, then set out to pay their parents back with a financial instrument called a Guaranteed Retained Annuity Trust. They agreed to pay $1.3 million to Brown Sr. and his wife Caroline in monthly installments. Another 25 percent of the stock went into Generation Retained Annuity Trust [GRAT], while the remaining 50 percent of the stock stayed with the parents. When their father died in 1995, his 25 percent went to his wife. The sons continued paying their mother for her 50 percent ownership until her death in 2007 when the remaining stock went to them, per terms of the GRAT. Their three siblings, sisters SuSu and Brenda and brother Bill, took possession of the groves their mother had inherited from her father, plus acreage Brown Sr., had acquired.

"At the time, it was an equitable deal," Gator said. "He struggled with it a lot because he wanted to be fair to all his kids."

The key, Gator said, was that his father was trying to ensure his wife would be well taken care of if he died first. "If she wants anything, it's hers. No questions asked," Gator said his father told him.

Caroline Brown succumbed to brain cancer eleven years after her husband died.


## CRASHING THE PROCESSED MEAT MARKET

The brothers loved their work through the years, but the stress was constant and growing exponentially, particularly after they found a way to dominate the lucrative and fast-growing natural portion of the international processed meat market. Producing, then selling, celery powder as both a natural flavor and a natural preservative, they were running up internal profit margins in excess of 50 percent. This in an industry where the standard margins were 6 to 8 percent.

Their client list was a *Who's Who* of the worldwide meat market: Boar's Head, Hormel, Cargill, Tyson, Hillshire, Applegate and others. The products ranged from bacon to beef jerky to lunch meats, even seafood and pet foods.

Gator often found himself waking up in the middle of the night, unable to fall back asleep, puzzling over a production or supply issue. He'd get on the computer, write himself notes on what to do when he went into work. Tom was worried, too.

"We needed help," Gator said. "We were all running so hard. We were all in, all the time. Weekends, it never ended."

They were reluctant to add staff or invest more heavily in the plant, leaving the brothers stretched too thin. "It was our money," Tom said of their aversion to expand. "We were probably too careful."

Gator added, "We were swapping Peter to pay Paul all the time, a constant juggling act between manpower and equipment."

It was inevitable, they knew, that stronger, bigger and more heavily capitalized companies eventually would realize just how profitable the food segment FFP controlled had become. And they would come after FFP, overwhelming the ability of the small business to compete and maintain market share.

## DECIDING TO SELL

So Gator and Tom talked long and hard before finally agreeing to sell during the fall of 2014. One of their first moves was hiring Simmons, whose expertise is in readying small to medium companies for sale. He tightened up the books and company procedures and pushed to get long-term, assignable contracts with clients. He became a key member of the transition team, meeting with Tom at least once a week to go over what was happening and where they were headed.

"I come in with a buyer's perspective." Simmons said, "and I help the company (seller) build their case." He likened the process to the unpleasant notion of heart surgery: "You know it's serious, but it's going to be a really good thing when it's over. But you have to do it."

Of Simmons, Gator said, "He prepped us for the big boys. He was an excellent choice."

Simmons also worked well with Edgar Anders, whom the brothers had hired three years earlier to be in charge of new product development. Anders excelled at presentations and Gator and Tom wanted to show the sum of FFP was more than just celery powder. "He brought some professionalism to us," Tom said of Anders.

The brothers then hired an investment banker, Tim Larsen of Houlihan Lokey, based in Chicago. Larsen, the managing director in Houlihan Lokey's consumer, food and retail group, started soliciting bids in 2015. The initial target audience was corporate buyers, or strategics, in sales parlance. The Browns and their advisors figured corporations would offer the most money because they would be more familiar with FFP and its business model. Months of negotiations back and forth followed.

Seven companies made bids by the end of 2015, each flying into Orlando International Airport, where FFP rented a conference room. Typically, the talks would last half a day. Spreadsheets analyzing each offer and comparing them were assembled. In the end, all were rejected as too low. The best offer was millions short of the hoped-for price.

"That was deflating," Tom said. "You decide you want to sell something, it's decided. It's going to be sold and I'm going to be out. It was a big letdown."

FFP was not an easy sell, Simmons said, because big companies are risk averse and did not understand the true import of what FFP had to offer. "Are they all going to be afraid of this baby?" Simmons said. "They just didn't understand the business."

Gator's summary: "Basically, nobody wanted us."

The brothers resolved to go back to work. "To heck with it," Gator said. "It's worth a whole lot more. Let's buckle down and grow it."

About four months later, during the spring of 2016, Larsen called back and said he had drummed up interest with private equity outfits. In fact, he said, he had as many as ten firms that wanted to talk, including the eventual winner Kainos Capital.

Three days of meetings were set at the airport with potential suitors, with one would-be buyer following another, as if on a conveyor belt. Tom and Gator rarely spoke during the sessions, even though it was their livelihood that was on the line. They preferred letting Simmons, Anders and Larsen make the case.

Gator described the process as similar to peeling away the layers of an onion. The more questions and interest that the possible buyers asked and exhibited, the more information FFP would let loose.

The biggest knock against FFP was that roughly 70 percent of the income was generated by celery powder, meaning there was a lack of solid secondary products. In other words, in private equity eyes, FFP was a "one-trick pony." There also were concerns about a patent squabble, the up and down nature of the market, the transition from the Browns to a new set of leaders and questions about management depth.

The talks were not easy. The brothers had to listen as outsiders criticized and picked at their life's work. But they finally reached an agreement with Kainos, which is run by three partners and bills itself as a middle market private equity firm specializing in the consumer and food market. The Kainos partners, according to company literature, pride themselves on knowing about "every aisle of the grocery store." That background helped them understand what FFP was all about. The runner-up was Arbor Investments of Chicago.

One by one, each participant said yes, including Tom and Jerry, who goes by his childhood nickname of Gator. The call lasted less than fifteen minutes. And that was it. Sixty-two years of family history had come to an abrupt end for the brothers.

Gator hung up the phone, stared a moment at the white walls of his modest, largely nondescript office, then donned a parka, pulled up the hood and went outside. Immediately pelted by howling winds, his eyes misted and tears fell, mingling with the rain on his face as the finality of the call hit him. "That's it?" he thought. "Money's in the account. Party's over?"

Head down, body bowed against the gusts, Gator made his way about the grounds. He looked, as if for the first time, at the twelve buildings of various sizes and shapes that comprise FFP. The place had been expanded and remodeled continually over the years, yet the original core remained, including one building that dated back to 1946, eight years before his father and business associates bought the property.

"I'm walking around and thinking, 'This isn't our's anymore,'" recalled Gator, who had started for good at FFP in 1980, two years after graduating from the University of Florida. He was sorely conflicted, relieved that the sale had gone through, ending an arduous, emotional two-year process. Yet, he was almost grief stricken. A major link to his father was gone. Though well compensated, his life's calling had ended. He had been cut adrift. "You can't sell yourself," Gator said of the Kainos transaction. "You're gone."

Conversely, Tom felt little emotionally, even though he, too, had spent his entire professional career at FFP, joining the company in 1983, one year after graduating from Florida State University. "You work, work, work, then you close. It didn't overwhelm me," he said.

A few days later, after Matthew had come ashore in South Carolina and dissipated, the brothers went back to the property. As the sun fell, they sat under a tree and knocked back a couple of shots of Early Times whiskey, their father's drink of choice.

"It was terrible," Gator chuckled in describing the Early Times taste, though he could have just as easily been talking about the emotional turmoil the sale caused him.

"Seemed anticlimactic," Tom said. "It kind of happens and you move on."

Regardless of the money involved, the deal brought an end to more than six decades of Browns walking the grounds of Florida Food Products, talking to and directing employees, making deals and meeting deadlines, sweating over details large and small. The place they spent countless hours working no longer belonged to them, as Gator realized as the winds of Hurricane Matthew bore down on him.

"Sometimes," Gator said, "I still can't believe it's over."

## THE BOG WORLD

### FIRES, FREEZES AND LIFE BEFORE AIR
### CONDITIONING

**B**lack Lake Park looks like countless other gated subdivisions in Central Florida. Developed in 2005, the houses are box-like, the exterior stucco and wood frequently painted a light pastel, the roofs often a rusty brown. The lots are uniform and the front yards typically boast a palm tree or two, sidewalks lining either side of the asphalt streets. The main distinguishing feature is a park with a gazebo and flagpole that faces the main entrance. At the base of the pole, which flies the Stars and Stripes, is a plaque that reads, in part, "Dedicated to the family of Phil C. Peters.

Few, if any, Black Lake Park residents likely know who Phil Christian Peters was or the impact he and his extended family had on the state, the region and Winter Garden, the now trendy town of cafes and shops that sits five miles to the north and is traversed by a popular bike path that daily draws a wide array of cyclists, runners and walkers.

Go back in time forty, sixty — try one hundred and thirty

— years and the Peters clan was among the most prominent members of an era and place unrecognizable to the people who now call Black Lake Park or Winter Garden home. People who couldn't tell the difference between a Valencia or a Hamlin, two varieties of oranges that once proliferated throughout the region, even on what are now neatly manicured St. Augustine lawns routinely fertilized every spring and fall.

The Peterses were, to put it simply, a big deal. They were instrumental not only in the development of the citrus industry — next to tourism perhaps the biggest business and employer Florida had during much of the twentieth century — but the social fabric of Winter Garden, then the epicenter of the orange trade.

The family first came to what is Black Lake Park during the late 1880s, moving from Belleville, Illinois, where the Peterses had immigrated from Germany earlier during the century. They left the Midwest to escape the harsh winters and start anew in a part of Florida that was sparsely populated and known as much for its mosquitoes as it was a respite from snow and ice. Back then, what is now Orange County was called Mosquito County.

Phil C. Peters was eight at the time and his father figured the warm weather would be good for his wife, Caroline, who was in poor health. Phil was the only boy in a family that included five girls: Carrie, Emma, Alma, Drucilla and Catherine. The children were all first-generation Americans.

The family and hired hands carved ninety acres out of the oak and pine trees and scrub starting near the east end of Black Lake, claiming it as Peters' land through a collection of laws commonly referred to as the federal Homestead Acts.

Over time, they planted by seed a citrus grove, oranges that eventually were crossbred and refined into Hamlins that ripen from October to December and Valencias that could be picked during the spring and early summer. There were twenty five feet between the trees and each row.

Some eighty years later, the three teenage boys descended from the Peterses — Jerry, Bill and Tom Brown — would toil in those very same groves, pulling weeds and pruning, usually as punishment for misbehaving.

The trio would become well acquainted with the property, where workers hired by their great grandfather used the native woods to build a two-story home, which burned down within a few years, the cause of the blaze uncertain.

A second two-story house was built a bit north of the original home, again using native pines that provided everything from the rafters to the floor boards. The house stood in the middle of the property, away from the lake, which was standard practice then. Lakefronts were havens for mosquitoes and rife with alligators and other forms of unpredictable wildlife. Even with the separation from Black Lake, gators occasionally made their way to the yard around the main home, though no one recalls any dangerous encounters with the reptiles.

The second family home burned down, too, years later, the conflagration sparked by a lightning strike. The Peterses had not lived in the place since the late 1960s, the property inherited by Caroline and Freck. They rented the house, but the boarders were out when the fire started.

Several smaller wood houses were built on The Bog, too, mainly for the help, many of African descent. One structure close to the main house became the home of Arthur and Ida

Faircloth, a black couple who worked their entire lives for the Peterses.

## OLD PHOTOS HARKEN TO ANOTHER TIME

Black and white photos that are faded and losing their contrast attest to the lives they all led, lives that in their simplicity and lack of modern convenience seem almost unfathomable now. The pictures are sealed behind clear cellophane in a thick green book with a simple circular tab on the cover saying, "Old Family Album."

There are pictures of babies, toddlers and the elderly, of a Confederate captain and black workers, and of Phil Peters and his wife Margaret, or Maggie, in various stages of their lives, plus their two daughters, Caroline and Frances.

Many of the photos predate air conditioning, which historians generally credit with making Florida habitable year round. Willis Carrier of New York invented air conditioning in 1902, but nearly five decades passed before the average Florida home started sporting window units during the 1950s. Central air came on during the 1960s. For decades, air conditioning was one of the ways movie theaters, motels and restaurants appealed to potential customers seeking relief from the state's relentless heat and humidity.

Without air conditioning, Florida likely would have remained a backward locale populated by the hardy willing to live with the harsh summer conditions and seasonal types who wintered in the state, then returned to the Midwest or Northeast when the damp ninety-degree days returned by late spring.

Phil C. Peters is remembered by one of his four grandsons, Jerry Brown Jr., as a stern man of proud German descent who was intimidating to the youngsters who would visit the home and property that was known as "The Bog". "He was pretty stoic, quiet," said Brown Jr., known ad Gator from his early years.

Phil Cudahy, who lived on the property as a child, recalls her grandfather much differently. She said he was "extremely fair and kind and generous." Cudahy, whose parents expected her to be a boy, was named after Phil C. Peters. Her mother was Frances "Freck" Peters McGehee, the older daughter of the Peters. Their younger daughter, Caroline, was the mother of Jerry Brown Jr., two other sons and two daughters. Caroline was named after Phil C. Peters' mother.

Cudahy recalls lots of animals roaming about The Bog during the 1940s, including feral cats, ducks, chickens and a white mule named Queen.

The house was square in style, with a large, open front porch and a fountain beyond the front door. A rock garden was in a side yard. The home was painted white, with green trim. Sitting at the end of a long driveway that was lined with palm trees, the house was built two to three feet off the ground to improve air flow, making the heat a tad more tolerable. The second floor had a long sleeping porch — later enclosed with glass — built on the east side to avoid the heat of the setting sun. There were lots of windows, twelve-foot ceilings, plus a large, loud attic fan to suck the hot air out and cool the place off during the long, boiling summers.

"You didn't know what you were missing. You learned to

live with the heat," Cudahy said of growing up without air conditioning.

Like many old Florida cracker houses, the main home of The Bog was added onto and modified over time, with an indoor kitchen, bathrooms, entrance hall and other rooms, as well as the all-important installation of air conditioning.

The Peterses often tried to escape the torrid summers by staying at a house on a bluff overlooking Daytona Beach, about seventy miles from Winter Garden on Florida's East Coast. They would bask in the ocean breezes after taking their mattresses from The Bog over to the beach place, Cudahy said.

Cudahy's parents married during World War II after a short courtship. Her father, Capt. Tom McGehee, was a U.S. Army pilot who flew 179 hours worth of combat missions in B-17 Flying Fortresses during the war, military records show. McGehee became the squadron commander in the 305th Bombardment Group, Eighth Air Force. Serving in that group meant you had a 19 percent chance of dying during the war, according to the Quora website, which bills itself as a "place to share knowledge and better understand the world."

Cudahy spent many summers and much of her early years with her maternal grandparents because her father was overseas or on other military assignments. McGehee eventually became a three-star general and vice commander of the Aerospace Defense Command, Ent Air Force Base, Colorado. The command oversaw all U.S. Air Force aerospace defense resources to defend North America, except Alaska.

She loved living at her grandparents' home, which sloped down to Black Lake, where the surrounding grounds were wet and spongy. Often, she would tag along with her grandfather as he walked and inspected the citrus trees that surrounded the house on the higher, drier soil.

Grandfather, or Daddy Phil, as she called him, taught her to play solitaire, which she does to this day. He often played during the evening in the formal dining room of the main house. He loved to laugh with his granddaughter, she said.

"Bullbat time" was the colloquialism at the Peters house for when the adults would gather during the early evening hours for cocktails and a smoke on the first-floor porch. They would watch the martins coming home to roost, Cudahy said. Years later, Caroline and Jerry Brown would do the same at their home at the Orlando Country Club.

## EARLY STRUGGLES FOR PHIL C. PETERS

Peters was well established in the citrus industry during those years. But he had plenty of struggles getting to a point of prominence. He moved away from Black Lake after completing the eighth grade to work in South Georgia sawmills, according to articles in the *Orlando Sentinel*. Though he often came home for visits, he also spent time in South Florida, laboring in tomato fields there. He returned to The Bog for good in 1916, when he bought out his retiring father's share of the orange groves, the *Sentinel* reported.

One year earlier, in 1915, Peterses had married Margaret Sims. He was thirty-two, she was twenty-four and they had courted for three years. She was from a small town called Statenville, a bit south and east of Valdosta, Georgia. She lived there with an older sister, Minnie Staten, who went by the name "Aunt Sunshine." Family lore has it that the town was named in honor of the Staten clan.

Margaret also lived with another sister in Tampa and they were visiting relatives in Ocoee when she first met Peters. One of the founding fathers of the then-fledgling west Orange County town near Winter Garden was an uncle of Margaret: former Confederate Capt. Bluford M. Sims. Known as Uncle B to family, he was a teacher by trade. Sims had moved to Ocoee after the Civil War ended and operated the first commercial citrus nursery in the country, according to the *"History of Orange County Florida Narrative and Biographical,"* by William Fremont Blackman.

Caroline Peters Brown, in her memoir *Orange Blossom Petals*, described her mother as petite, barely five feet tall. Maggie Peters, Caroline Brown wrote, was not much of a chef or housekeeper, relying instead on the help, particularly Ida Faircloth for cooking and Arthur Faircloth for labor and gardening.

"Not only was she (Ida) great with good ole' Southern food but Mother...showed her how to cook and serve great gourmet meals," Caroline Brown wrote. Ida's breakfasts, Caroline Brown continued, were bountiful: "Freshly squeezed orange juice (fruit from the grove), oatmeal (cooked forever) with thick fresh cream that went plop when you poured it and the lightest, fluffiest muffins ever, served with pale churned butter, honey or homemade guava jelly. Of course, all of this was with your choice of eggs with bacon or ham."

Arthur, she wrote, often worked outside with her mother: "Her garden was one of her greatest joys. There, she and Arthur spent many hours where the roses were planted, where pansies, daisies, sweet peas and snapdragons were a burst of color in the spring." The flowers drew a host of hummingbirds and butterflies.

Caroline did not recall her parents fighting much, in part because Maggie "could wind Daddy around her little finger and did quite often. They both had a great sense of humor and really seemed to have fun together. Of course, there were disagreements between them, but Freck and I were never aware of unpleasant arguments."

The Peterses often hosted parties and were very involved in Winter Garden social and civic activities. In 1936, the *Sentinel* wrote, Maggie Peters was in charge of raising $125,000 to build the Winter Garden Memorial Hospital. During that same year, she helped found the West Orange Junior Service League. Six years later, during April 1942, she opened a recreation center in the Edgewater Hotel in downtown Winter Garden for area servicemen. She also was a member of the Women's Club of Winter Garden executive board, 1926 through 1927.

Winter Garden, now the third largest city in Orange County with nearly 39,000 residents and a bustling downtown, was a quiet, modest place during much of the twentieth century. Just a few thousand people called it home during the early and mid-1900s, when the Peters family was ascendent and a major force in the community. There wasn't much of a middle class and the largest share of the population was engaged directly in citrus, either the growing or harvesting ends, or in related jobs, such as fertilizer or farm equipment sales.

Mount Dora attorney and lifelong Lake County resident Frank Gaylord said there wasn't much money in the region during those times. "Back then, there were grove owners, professionals and everybody else," Gaylord said. "It was tough to make a living."

## PETERS WAS A CITRUS TITAN

That confluence of factors made Peters a force in town. Caroline Brown recalled her father as a "strong man, both physically and mentally. Yes, and morally, too." He stood just under six foot, though she wrote he appeared to be a much larger man. He taught Sunday School for many years at the Winter Garden Methodist Church and was generous with his time and contributions to the parish.

In addition to the citrus groves he owned and worked for seventy-six years, Peters became manager of the Winter Garden Citrus Growers Association in 1931. He guided the organization — one of the most prominent citrus cooperatives in the state — for the next thirty-two years. He championed high quality standards for fresh fruit products and he helped found a leading juicing cooperative in Winter Garden Citrus Products during 1943, becoming the organization's first vice president. When orange juice concentrate was introduced to Florida during the late 1940s, Peters helped to make the organization one of Florida's largest processors. He also served on the Florida Citrus Commission from 1938 through 1939, the Florida Citrus Exchange from 1955 to 1962 and was one of the leading organizers of the growers cooperative Florida Citrus Mutual.

A *Sentinel* article listed him in the Who's Who of Citrus in 1941, saying: "That a citrus grove is like a factory, Phil Peters of

Winter Garden has made a success of citrus growing. A citrus grove manufactures oranges just as an automobile factory makes cars. And you have to treat the trees more carefully than the fine machinery." For reasons lost to time, Peters greatly disliked grapefruit.

An April, 1944 edition of *Citrus Magazine* credited Peters with steadily increasing the membership and production of the Winter Garden Citrus Growers Association. The association's vice president, B.D. Bennett, said "Phil's ability to see things coming and to always be prepared for eventualities" was key to the organization's success.

Peters, who assiduously promoted the association orange brands of Crane and Bull Frog, said he was ready to retire when he stepped down in 1963. It was time, he said, for someone younger to take the reins.

He was inducted into the Florida Citrus Hall of Fame in 1973, five years after his death from old age. His wife preceded him in death, falling to a bout of pneumonia. Family lore, Cudahy said, has it that Maggie knew her husband was failing and that she succumbed to her illness rather than fighting it because she knew Phil Peters would soon join her in the hereafter. "She just gave up," Cudahy said.

In *Orange Blossom Petals,* Caroline wrote that life on The Bog was near idyllic, sounding almost like being raised on Tara, the imaginary plantation in the classic Civil War novel *Gone With The Wind.* Caroline said she and her sister Freck flourished and frolicked on The Bog. They used to jump out of a barn on the west side of the house onto a haystack or, better yet, their ponies, Dimple and Dot. The animals were a surprise Christmas present for the girls after their parents went on a vacation in Kentucky and made the purchase, along with a fringe-topped surrey.

"We were delighted and surprised little girls," she wrote.

Caroline Brown recalled hitching Dimple to the surrey and "taking off through the groves toward the small settlement of Gotha, only to come across a rather large ditch. There, Dimple leaped into the air, swinging me and the surrey sky high, only to get half way over and land in the muddy water."

Dimple provided some of her fondest memories. "The very best rides were in the spring, when the groves burst with blossoms," she wrote, adding she loved the freedom that riding the pony brought to her as a youngster.

Often, the sisters would be in the yard and call out for Arthur, who was nowhere in sight, but would appear, as if by magic. "He would come and laugh with us and then saddle the ponies," she said. "Barn activities also included climbing up on its tin roof, sliding down to land on the grass below, provided, of course, that the scorching sun had not made the slide too hot for our precious little backsides."

| Ponies Dimple and Dot defined early days in the Bog

Another beloved Christmas present was a virtually life-size playhouse for the girls. It was ten feet by ten feet, painted white with green trim — like the main house — and featured double-hung windows and a front porch. It was placed in a side yard.

"On that first Christmas morning after it was built, we were surprised to find the playhouse totally furnished with little tables and chairs, a little cupboard with a tea set, cooking utensils and a little stove," she wrote of the structure that eventually was moved to the Orlando home where she raised her five children. It became a make-believe fort for her rambunctious youngsters.

## ORANGES INTEGRAL TO PETERS

Citrus, Caroline wrote, was always a part of her life. She was born in the middle of an orange grove on June 24, 1920, in the midst of the spring blooming season. Her father actually helped deliver her because the doctor could not drive the fifteen miles from Orlando to The Bog in time to tend to the very pregnant Maggie. "When the doctor did finally arrive, it is said that Daddy met him at the door with a few choice words!"

Weather was a constant concern, too. "It was seldom just right, Either it was too hot or too cold, too wet or too dry, and seldom was it just right." The Peters family lived through numerous freezes, stretching back to when they first settled the property. One cold snap, just before the turn of the twentieth century, killed not only the fruit, but many trees as well.

"Daddy would tell us about the early hard freeze when the sap caused the trunks and limbs of the trees to burst, about how many of the families left their groves in Central Florida and moved to South Florida," she wrote. According to Florida

Citrus Mutual, there were freezes in 1899, 1917, 1934, 1940, 1957 and 1962 while the Peters family was living at The Bog. The 1899 snap was particularly harsh, with Orlando recording an extended low of twenty degrees. Once temperatures drop below twenty-eight degrees for four or more hours, tree damage is likely.

"I came to realize that being connected with the citrus business was like rolling dice. The old saying, 'You win some, you lose some.' Yet the growers and their families usually rolled with the punches," she wrote.

Before the advent of concentrated orange juice, fruit that had been frozen by cold weather was worthless, left to rot on the trees and fall to the ground, destroying an entire year's worth of work. "The trees, with their molding, rotting fruit, like white skirts around their trunks, took on a sad look, while a musty sweet odor blanketed the countryside," she recounted.

Growers often would tend fires, igniting wood or old tires, to fend off the cold. The Bog had a bit more protection from low temperatures than many locations because it was warmed by Lake Apopka to the north and, closer to home, Black Lake.

Caroline and Freck, who was the oldest by sixteen months, went to elementary school and high school in Winter Garden. Caroline became a running center on the high school girls basketball team, a cheerleader and the first homecoming queen. The *Sentinel* referred to her in one story as "a popular member of the younger set."

Caroline summed up the high school years by writing, "I was a pretty good student and Freck was an excellent one, so upon graduation off we went to Virginia to college."

They both graduated from Hollins College in Roanoke,

though Freck would have preferred going to the Florida State College for Women with her friends. Both did well at Hollins, with Freck graduating ahead of her sister, then heading back to The Bog.

Caroline, who would be voted Hollins class president, had just returned to her dorm room from the library and was visiting with her two roommates when she heard yelling down the hallway, "The Japs have attacked Pearl Harbor!" The date was December 7, 1941.

## PEARL HARBOR CHANGES EVERYTHING

"From that minute on," Caroline wrote, "our lives changed. No longer were we college girls without a care, thinking only about a date or exam. The entire school was feeling a shock wave. All the girls were calling home, trying to contact their families (some of whom were in military service) and get in touch with boyfriends, wherever they were."

The war created another "bombshell" a little more than a year later, when McGehee proposed to Freck. "She called me to say that she was going to marry a young Air Force captain who was at the time stationed at the Orlando Air Force Base. I was pretty upset because she had just met him a month or so before and had only dated him a few times."

A May wedding date was set, but with a caveat. McGehee had been transferred to Salt Lake City and he asked the father of the bride if the wedding could be held there. "Daddy's reply to that was 'If that young man is a captain, which I doubt, he can surely come down here for the wedding,'" Caroline wrote.

The nuptials occurred in Winter Garden and, a short while

later, McGehee was shipped off to Europe to fight in the war. Caroline graduated in the spring of 1942 and returned to The Bog after a short stay in Atlanta spent fruitlessly seeking a job. Feeling deflated, but with a psychology degree in hand, Caroline started looking about Orlando for work.

Rationing was in full swing, with sugar and gasoline, even shoes, in short supply. Gas was no problem because The Bog had an agricultural exemption. Caroline wrote she was not averse to driving about to beat back the boredom. Freck returned to The Bog with baby Phil Sharon McGehee in tow because her husband was bombing the Nazis. The sisters would read the papers and huddle around the radio, listening for any scrap of news or update on the war.

By this time, Ensign Alexander Z "Jerry" Brown of the U.S. Navy was writing letters to Caroline. "These V-mails were pretty poor excuses for letters, since they were written on flimsy thin paper and were about the size of note paper," Caroline wrote. "Not only that, it took weeks for V-mail to arrive and when it did, it often had long black marks over words or sentences that the censors had deleted for security purposes. One V-mail from Jerry was almost totally black!"

Caroline went to USO events in Orlando to dance with soldiers who were stationed at a nearby Signal Corp camp and she rolled bandages as a volunteer. She also would sit in a wooden "spotting tower" scanning the skies for enemy planes. All she saw, she wrote, were buzzing mosquitoes.

Then she landed a job with Dickson & Ives, one of downtown Orlando's two major department stores. She became the assistant to the advertising manager, laying out newspaper ads, writing merchandise descriptions and planning fashion shows.

"It truly was fun," wrote Caroline, who eventually succeeded the ad manager when he left to start his own business.

"Looking back," she wrote, "the war years were like an island, unique unto itself. All of the events of my life were chronicled by a time frame...before the war, after the war."

She tried not to dwell on the acquaintances she lost during the great conflict. "I can only thank God that our own family and close friends did not suffer a personal loss," she wrote.

Life changed dramatically after the war ended and the veterans came home, looking for jobs, hoping to pick up where they left off, or, in the case of Caroline and Jerry Brown, taking their relationship to a different level.

"Jerry and I had gone to high school together and even though we had dated when he came home on leave from the Navy, now things started to become more serious!" she wrote.

Caroline did not mention in her book that her beau had been telling his friends that he knew she would be his bride the day he first laid eyes on her. That was back at Lakeview High School in Winter Garden, where she was a couple of years ahead of him and he was a star athlete in football and basketball.

They had little to no interaction prior to high school because they came from two entirely different parts of town. She was south of Winter Garden, living amongst the groves, while Brown was just off the main drag, in a small frame home.

She came from a well-to-do family; he did not. But the war, as Caroline wrote, changed everything. His social and economic status meant little once the war ended. He was a University of Florida graduate, a vet, a man ready to make and take his place in the world.

Brown moved through a succession of jobs during his first three years out of the service, knowing he wanted to be his own boss at some point. After hiring on at a sales position with a citrus concentrate plant in Dade City, he decided, in Caroline's words, to start "a new venture...Me!"

They were married April 2, 1949 at the First Methodist Church in Winter Garden, where her father had taught Sunday School for years. Her sister Freck was the maid of honor and Phil (Cudahy) was the junior bridesmaid. It rained, but no one complained because they were in the midst of a drought and the orange trees were in dire need of water.

"Jerry," Caroline wrote, "was an ardent admirer of mother and agreed to all her plans for the affair, with only one exception: How his name would be printed on the invitation. When he suggested Alexander Z Brown, she commented that an initial just wasn't acceptable. Anyway, they compromised with Alexander Jerry Brown. Jerry laughingly said, "All right, Miss Maggie, but it really isn't my name."

## UNSPOKEN WAR TRUTHS

### GRADUATED ONE DAY; ENLISTED THE NEXT

W orld War II was verging on disaster for the Allied Forces in 1942. The United States had finally joined the great conflict, though it was still reeling from the surprise, December 7, 1941 Japanese bombing of Pearl Harbor that virtually destroyed its battle fleet. The nation, quite simply, was woefully unprepared, its armed forces too small, its weaponry often outdated and undersized.

The German blitzkrieg had secured much of Europe, Northern Africa, the Middle East and South Pacific for the Fuhrer Adolf Hitler and the Axis powers of Germany, Italy and Japan. London and outlying British cities had been mercilessly bombed by the German Luftwaffe for more than a year. The Japanese had cornered 24,000 battered and starving American and Filipino soldiers on the Bataan Peninsula in the South China Sea and were moving in for the kill.

About the only good news for Americans during the first

half of that dismal year occurred when Lt. Col. Jimmy Doolittle and a squadron of sixteen B-25s lifted off from the aircraft carrier *USS Hornet* and bombed the Japanese cities of Nagoya, Tokyo, Kobe, Osaka and Yokohama. It was a moral victory, giving the folks back home something to brag about, but caused little damage to the enemy.

Two days after Doolittle's daring raid — on April 30, 1942 — a slender young man by the name of Alexander Z Brown caught a bus from Gainesville, Florida, to Jacksonville. Newly graduated from the University of Florida with a degree in accounting, his destination was the United States Navy recruitment center, where he intended to join the war effort.

He had worked his way through school by waiting on tables and washing dishes at the university cafeteria, obtaining his degree in only three years. Like countless other young men of what would later be dubbed "The Greatest Generation," Brown was ready, willing and able to fight. Could barely stand to wait, in fact.

He arrived at the center with three letters attesting to his good character. They were written by the minister of his Winter Garden church, Shuler Peele; the mayor of Winter Garden, L. F. Roper; and the owner of a prominent grocery and feed company, W.F. Cappleman.

"Mr. Brown is above the average in intelligence and ability. He possesses qualifications of a natural leader. He is industrious and his integrity is above question. He has a good background, coming from one of the community's best families," Cappleman wrote.

But, at twenty years old, he was too young by a year to enter the global fray for officer training on his own. So his mother, the widow Josephine Ellen McCombs Brown, signed the government papers that would put her only son in harm's way until he was discharged in February, 1946, changed forever by the horrors he would encounter in both the Atlantic and Pacific waters.

Brown, whose complexion was listed as ruddy on his enlistment papers, weighed 150 pounds and stood five feet ten inches. He had blue eyes and brown hair. A star athlete who lettered in football, basketball and baseball at his Winter Garden, Florida, high school, he went by the nickname Jerry, after a character in a popular comic strip called Jerry On The Job.

## STARTING PAY: TWENTY ONE DOLLARS A MONTH

He entered the Navy as an apprentice seaman, Class V-7. His pay was twenty-one dollars a month and, initially, he was considered a member of the Naval Reserve. Among his qualifications for the apprentice program were his college degree and his successful completion of a trigonometry class and other math studies.

Like all branches of the military at that time, the Navy was overrun with draftees and enlistees and it took a while for Brown to report for active duty and officer training. He was sent to Northwestern University in Chicago on March 9, 1943.

That made Brown a member of one of twenty five classes totaling 26,750 men who went through the apprentice program, including a future president of the United States – John F. Kennedy. Graduates often were referred to as "90-day wonders" because they came in as naive young men with no military experience and, after training, were suddenly officers whose decisions often could have life or death consequences.

By that time, the war was turning slightly in favor of the Allies, but was far from won. The Russians had defeated the Germans in the long, blood-soaked siege of Stalingrad and the Americans were retaking New Guinea from the Japanese and about to invade Sicily. But most of Europe, as well as much of the Middle East, North Africa and the Pacific, remained under Axis control.

While he anxiously waited to see action and before he went to Northwestern, Brown spent some time back at his modest home, 145 North Highlands Avenue, a brick road little more than a block off the main drag of Plant Street in downtown Winter Garden, which sat in the heart of Central Florida's expanding citrus belt. Brown lived with his mother, Josephine, and sister, Tex Amanda, who was four years older than Jerry.

Their two-bedroom, one-bath frame house — now an empty lot — was painted white with green trim and had no more than 1,000 square feet under roof. Brown slept in a rough addition attached to the one-car garage, which sat on the back of the lot. There was a single grapefruit tree in the yard.

His father, Alexander Z, and mother had moved to Winter Garden from North Florida, where they came from large families. Most of them had been tobacco farmers or extractors of turpentine from scrub pine trees. The turpentine was used as fuel in World War I. Between them, they had twenty four siblings. Among Mrs. Brown's brothers was a minister called "preachin' John" and an apparent underachiever called "drinkin' John" who lived on a farm.

Alexander Z died in 1934 of a heart attack while driving to the hospital after complaining that he felt ill. A fertilizer salesman by trade, he was fifty-four. That left Josephine in charge. She took a job as a secretary to bring in money. A strict Baptist, she lived the rest of her life on Highland Avenue, dying at eighty one from a blood clot that broke loose.

During the war, just a few thousand people lived in Winter Garden, almost all of them working in citrus, or jobs that were affiliated with the industry. It was a quintessential small Southern town, where few locked their doors and everyone knew everyone else's business, private and public. During those segregated times, whites lived where they pleased, while blacks were confined to a place referred to as the quarters. Almost all the jobs worked by people of color were at the pleasure of whites.

Most of Winter Garden's residents, regardless of race, were blue collar and not particularly well off financially. It was not unusual for boys to go to school barefoot, recalled Jerry Chicone, now a retired citrus grower who grew up on Highlands Avenue and would, in future years, be neighbors with Brown at two other locations.

"You didn't know who had anything and who didn't," Chicone said of the hardscrabble town.

Brown listed only his mother as his next of kin in his Navy documents and he sent his monthly check of $100 — his pay after being promoted to ensign — to her. He also deducted $18.75 each month to buy a $25 savings bond, his Naval records show.

There was no mention in his service papers of the woman he would eventually marry, Caroline Peters. They dated casually at Lakeview High School and corresponded during his time in the service. Two years his senior, Caroline Peters lived five miles south of Winter Garden on a ninety90-acre tract filled with citrus trees that had been homesteaded during the late 1880s by her grandfather Pete Peters.

Her father, Phil C. Peters, was a leader in citrus, once holding a seat on the influential Florida Citrus Commission. He probably was best known as the manager of the powerful Winter Garden Citrus Growers Association from 1931 to 1963. He died in 1973 at the age of eighty-four.

Caroline Peters was popular at Lakeview High and an athlete in her own right, playing basketball and cheerleading. She was named the school's first homecoming queen. But by her account, she and Brown were not romantically serious. That would change after he returned from the war.

Brown's first assignment was going to USS Midshipman School, where he came out as a gunnery officer. He also went to sub-chaser training in Miami for two months, followed by two months of schooling on amphibious tactics. By January of 1944, Jerry Brown was ready for the war and had become one of 4.2 million men and women who eventually would serve in the Navy before Germany, Japan and Italy finally surrendered.

## FIRST POST FOR BROWN WAS LAST FOR MANY

He was assigned to the *LST 507*, the initials LST being the Navy acronym for Landing Ship, Tanks. Sailors disparaged the vessels as Large, Slow Targets. The *507* stretched 322 feet from bow to stern and its maximum speed was twelve knots. Designed to carry men and heavy equipment and machines, it had a flat bottom for carrying cargo and was little more than a big welded box that floated. Its bow was flat, but slightly rounded, allowing it to go all the way onto a sandy beach, where the ramp could be lowered to disgorge men and their mechanized weaponry. It also carried Higgins boats, which would be hydraulically lowered off the side of the ship. Unwieldy and bulky were the kindest descriptions of an LST's maneuvering capabilities.

The LST 507 was designed more for transporting cargo than for maneuvering enemy waters.

The ship was built in Jeffersonville, Indiana, records show, and, on New Year's Day, 1944, started its maiden voyage by steaming down the Ohio River to the Mississippi, where it would dock in New Orleans. It was commissioned in the Big Easy before making its way through the Gulf of Mexico and across the Atlantic Ocean. It landed first at Rosemeath, Scotland, then motored south to Falmouth and Brixham Harbor, on the southwest English coast. Brixham became the 507's home port.

Located in rural County Devon, the area where Brown was stationed was known as the South Hams. Two of its main attractions for the Allies were unpredictable, often harsh, weather and a sloping, pebble-filled beach about three miles long called Slapton Sands. Once off the beach, the ground rose dramatically into forested hills and bluffs. In short, it resembled what was referred to as Utah Beach at Normandy, where the Allies were secretly planning to launch a massive invasion of France within a few months.

Americans had been training in the South Hams for more than a year when Brown arrived. The British military had previously evacuated roughly 3,000 people from their homes and property in a twenty-five-square-mile region to make way for what came to be known as the "American Army Battle School."

One of numerous training maneuvers launched from the harbor was disastrous and almost cost Brown his life. Others were not so lucky. Nearly 640 men perished in an incident called Exercise Tiger, an operation that was so catastrophic the military kept it a secret for fear of damaging morale and tipping the enemy to the imminent D-Day invasion. Many records were kept classified for four decades. Survivors were threatened with court martials if they spoke of what happened.

On the evening of April 27, 1944, a joint command of the British and Americans decided to stage of mock invasion of

Slapton Sands, substituting for Utah Beach at Normandy. They sent a flotilla of eight LSTs — including the *507*, on which Brown was assigned — out into the English Channel to simulate the crossing they would endure on D-Day.

Fully loaded with soldiers and equipment, the LSTs were supposed to return to Slapton Sands during the early morning, emptying the men, trucks, tanks and various paraphernalia onto the beach. They were to be greeted with live ammunition fired over their heads to give them an idea of the deafening noise, mayhem and resistance they would face.

The *507* carried almost 500 soldiers and sailors, plus it was jammed with amphibious DUKWs (six-wheel armored vehicles capable of floating), jeeps, tanks and trucks in the cargo hold. The *507* was in a second group of three LSTs, last in line. Another group of five left from nearby Plymouth. They met up in the channel.

## FROM REVELRY TO DEADLY IN AN INSTANT

The atmosphere aboard the *507* was lax, almost like a cruise, according to the book *Exercise Tiger* by Nigel Lewis, which was published in 1990 and recounted the deadly event through military records and interviews with survivors. There were no drills as the vessels moved out to sea, including abandon ship or how the soldiers were to put life jackets on over their bulky uniforms and equipment. Instead, many of the men lolled about the ships, laughing and playing cards and singing along with guitars, banjos, clarinets and harmonicas.

Called the T-4, the convoy of LSTs chugged away from land at five to six knots. The sea was calm, visibility was good and a quarter moon was low and setting, according to succinct recounting of the event in a report written a week later by Lt. J. F. Murdock.

The convoy was oblivious to the fact that four German E-boats known as *Schnellbootes* were on patrol. The fast, highly mobile E-boats were similar to, but mightier than, the American PT boats made famous during the 1963 movie *PT 109*, about a doomed ship captained by future president Kennedy during the war in the South Pacific.

The T-4 moved east in an inexplicable, easy-to-attack straight line, the book said. The LSTs were supposed to be protected by two warships, one a small craft called a corvette, the other a World War 1 destroyer. But the destroyer bumped into an LST earlier in the day and remained behind in port for repairs, leaving the T-4 virtually defenseless.

The E-boats, on random patrol, picked up on the radio traffic between the Allied ships and quickly moved into position. The attack began shortly after 1 a.m., April 28. At first, the Americans were slow to react, thinking tracer bullets they saw streaking across the sky were part of the practice run. But soon enough, they knew they were in trouble. They were eighteen miles from port.

Lt. Eugene Eckstam, the *507*'s doctor, has an account of what he experienced posted on the internet. "I remember hearing gunfire and saying they had better watch where they were shooting or someone would get hurt," he wrote. "At 0203 I was stupidly trying to go topside to see what was going on and suddenly "BOOM!" There was a horrendous noise accompanied by the sound of crunching metal and dust everywhere. The lights went out and I was thrust violently in the air to land

on the steel deck on my knees, which became very sore immediately thereafter. Now I knew how getting torpedoed felt. But
I was lucky."

Last in the convoy line, the 507 had been struck in the
auxiliary engine room, essentially the heart of the ship. All
electrical and water power was gone. Fire erupted and quickly
spread. The 507 was unable to return fire at the Germans,
Murdock's report said.

"We sat and we burned," Eckstam wrote, adding that most
of the men had scrambled to the top deck of the 507 after the
initial explosion.

"The tank deck (below) was a different matter. As I opened
the hatch, I found myself looking into a raging inferno which
pushed me back. It was impossible to enter. The screams and
cries of those many Army troops in there still haunt me.
Navy regulations call for dogging (closing) the hatches to
preserve the integrity of the ship, and that's what I did."

— LT. EUGENE ECKSTAM

After that, he wrote, "We watched the most spectacular
fireworks ever. Gas cans and ammunition exploding and the
enormous fire blazing only a few yards away are sights forever
etched in my memory."

Adding to the mayhem was the fact that the numerous
landing crafts on the ship called Higgins boats could not be
launched because the 507 had lost power. The boats, if released
from the 507, could have saved countless lives, surmised the

late Ken Small, who wrote a book about the disaster called *The Forgotten Dead.*

Seaman Second Class Steve Sadlon worked the radios on the 507 and wrote on the Exercise Tiger website that, "I was thrown out of my chair by the concussion from the exploding torpedo. My head hit the overhead bulkhead and knocked me out. One of the radio transmitters that was as large as a refrigerator toppled to the floor beside where I was sprawled. When I woke up after the torpedo hit us, I staggered from the radio shack through a companion way into the wheelhouse. All of the ship's officers were gathered in the wheelhouse. All hell was breaking loose aboard ship. Fire was everywhere, ammunition as well as gas cans were exploding. Sailors were running all over the place."

## MAYHEM DEFINED THE NIGHT

Brown was among those in the wheelhouse with the captain of the ship, Lt. James Swarts, who would die that night. Brown later wrote a letter in long hand describing what happened that night to the father of Swarts. The paper is yellowed now and crinkly to the touch, but the black ink remains legible. Words and sentences sometimes are crossed out as Brown tried to find the right phrase or best way to ease the anguished mind of the elder Swarts.

"At the time we were hit, the Captain was on his bridge. He stayed there giving orders and doing everything that could possibly have been done to save his ship, until flames drove him to the stern. When it became apparent that nothing else could be done, he gave the order and personally directed abandon ship."

— JERRY BROWN

Brown did not mention his role during the chaos of the ship sinking, though he certainly played a part in trying to keep panic among the crew and soldiers from spreading while at the side of Swarts.

"I can assure you that through his guidance, there was an orderly abandon ship. The confidence shown him by the men in this extreme emergency is unbelievable," Brown wrote.

Before long, Brown continued, the only men left on board were himself, Swarts, two officers and two wounded soldiers. Swarts, "without hesitating or without thought of his own life," gave his life jacket to one of the wounded, according to Brown.

Left out of his account is the fact that Brown also gave away his life jacket to another. That decision, Brown Sr., decided in retrospect, likely saved his life, too, because he was forced to swim when he was in the water, keeping him warm enough to stave off hypothermia. Those were among the few details he shared about Exercise Tiger with his family.

Swarts then went about the sinking, smoke-filled and burning LST to make sure no one was still on board. He saw none. "In true Navy tradition," Brown wrote, "and being the captain that he was, he abandoned ship, the last person to leave."

Once in the black, mercilessly cold water, Brown, Swarts and others saw a raft, but it was near a slick of burning oil and gasoline. Another ensign, Frederick O. Beattie, swam under the flames, and retrieved the raft, Brown wrote to Navy superiors in an attempt to win Beattie a commendation. The wounded were placed in the raft, while the able-bodied clung to its sides.

"Had he not done this," Brown wrote of Beattie, "I am sure none of us would have survived." It is unclear if Beattie was awarded a commendation.

Sadlon recalled swimming around fire and floating bodies until he drifted to a place that seemed relatively safe: "I quieted down and my flotation belt slipped up under my arms. My head fell back on one shoulder and kept my face out of the water as hypothermia started taking control of my body in the forty-two degree water. Just before I passed out, I can remember seeing my mother's face. She was holding me in her arms and protecting me. I was a little kid again."

While the *507* was going down, the LSTs *531* and *289* also were hit by torpedoes, creating "a red-hot glow on the water," according to one sailor quoted in *Exercise Tiger*. The *531* sank within six minutes, while the *289*, its sailors and soldiers battling a blaze that crippled the ship, made it back to Slapton Sands.

The book also recounts how Brown was trying to paddle the raft retrieved by Beattie. "He was on a side," the book said of Brown. "Two were inside, with five others holding on. They were spotted by a shipmate, Tom Clark, who was clinging to a piece of wood."

"That you, Brownie?" Clark asked.

"Yes."

"Have you got the captain?"

"Yes, he's here, Tommy."

"Got room for one more?"

"Damn tootin', come on over."

After an hour in the icy water, eleven men had collected around the raft, Brown wrote.

"From then on," Brown's letter said, "it was a matter of waiting."

But time was not a friend to the survivors, as Sadlon had recounted.

## HYPOTHERMIA CLAIMS LIVES

"After we had been in the water about two hours," Brown wrote, "we began losing strength. First, two Army men lost consciousness, then the captain and another officer. They were all put inside the raft so their faces would not fall in the water and some first aid could be given."

By around 4 a.m., a fog rolled in, the air acrid, stinking of smoke and burning fuel. The sea was bobbing with corpses wearing Mae West life jackets, many face down in the water because they had not put them on properly. It was eerily quiet, a stark contrast to the cries, screams and concussive sounds of battle that had filled the air earlier.

"The soldiers that jumped or dove in with full packs did not do well," Eckstam wrote. "Most were found with their heads in the water and their feet in the air, top heavy from not putting the belts around their chests before inflating them. Instructions in their correct use had never been given."

Brown and his group were rescued by the *LST 515*, which had doubled back for survivors, even though the ship was under orders to head for shore because the higher-ups did not want to lose any more men or equipment before the invasion. The ExerciseTiger website credited the *515* with saving 134 men from the freezing water. The *515's* captain John Doyle, was threatened with court martial by a superior officer, but it was later withdrawn.

"The captain (Swarts of the 507) died from exposure shortly after he was taken aboard the rescue vessel," Brown wrote. "Although I was receiving medical attention myself, I know that every possible thing was done to save his life. I think that under the circumstances there was nothing that he or anyone else could have done to prevent his death."

Eckstam, was trained to wear his life belt properly, was picked up by the *515*, too. He had been drifting in the water for hours, barely holding onto life.

"I recall only brief moments of hearing motors, of putting a knee on a small boat ramp, and then 'awakening' half way up a Jacobs ladder...I had been in the water over 2 hours fully dressed and insulated.," Eckstam wrote. "Those that had stripped to swim, only God knows where they died. Drowning and hypothermia were the two major causes of death. I often wonder if many 'dead' victims were really in a state of hibernation, and what would have happened had we been able to immerse them in warm tubs. But who ever heard of a tub on an LST in wartime? We couldn't even do a reliable physical exam under the circumstances."

Dale Rodman, an *LST 507* survivor, was quoted in the *Daily Telegraph* of London as saying, "The worst memory I have is setting off in the lifeboat away from the sinking ship and watching bodies float by."

Sadlon said he woke up "lying on a mess table in the crew's quarters with 10 Army blankets over me. A corpsman patted me on the shoulder and said, 'You are a lucky guy. We were piling up dead people from your ship and you were foaming at the mouth. So we picked you up and started working on you'."

In his letter, Brown tried to console Swarts' father by saying his son's death was "not unpleasant. When we first entered the water, it was very cold, but then we got used to it. You could feel your strength wane. The end is very easy, without any suffering."

Brown also wrote that Swarts had the respect of every man on the LST 507: "It is impossible for me to explain my feelings toward the captain...He met and dealt with every problem fairly and squarely...He commanded a happy ship."

## BROWN SEEKS TO CONSOLE

Brown wrote a second letter as well, this one to the wife and son of another fallen comrade that he referred to only by his first name. "I have thought of you both quite often since that tragic night," he wrote to Dottie and Donnie. "I think it is needless to say that Chief Ken was my best friend aboard." There are two Navy men from the *507* listed as dying during

ExerciseTiger with the first name of Ken; one whose last name was Smith, the other Scott.

After the torpedo struck the *507*, Brown said he lost track of Ken, "but I do know that he was not wounded and got off the ship without injury. His death was caused by exposure."

Ken died, Brown wrote, in the same way as Swarts. It was not "unpleasant...At first you are cold, but from then on you become used to it and the end is like going asleep. The few of us that were saved were extremely lucky."

Brown then addressed Ken's son: "Donnie, your father was a great man. He was well liked by everyone that he met. There was absolutely nothing that his men wouldn't have done for him. He had great visions for you and knew that in being his son you will not disappoint him."

All told, 639 soldiers and sailors died the morning of April 28, 1944. Although counts of the dead vary, 194 men aboard the *507* are believed to have perished, with the rest of the casualties coming from the *531* and *289*. The five remaining LSTs and the corvette escort did not suffer any losses but were unable to return fire on the German E-boats, which escaped unscathed.

Brown and most of the other survivors were taken to an Army hospital in Sherborne, Dorset, not far from the South Hams. Like many military installations, it essentially was a bunch of metal Quonset-huts. The doctors, nurses and support staff were called together during the early morning of April 28th and told they soon would be treating men suffering from hypothermia and "explosion wounds." They were ordered not to talk about anything they saw or did upon threat of a court martial, according to the ExerciseTiger website.

Col. James Kendall, who commanded the hospital, told the hastily assembled gathering, "We're in the war at last."

Brown was examined and pronounced fit, with one minor exception. According to Brown family lore, one doctor told the shivering sailor that he likely was sterile after spending so much time in the frigid Channel water. Brown, who would pose in borrowed clothes for a black and white photo with other 507 survivors shortly after the exam, would prove the doctor wrong in coming years. His future wife Caroline Peters would bear five of his children, two girls and three boys.

Nearly 250 bodies were recovered from the water and transported to the Brookwood Cemetery in Surrey, about thirty miles southwest of London. Swarts' and Chief Ken's remains were among them. Swarts later was reinterred at Fort Bliss National Cemetery in El Paso, Texas at the request of his father, who was a Van Horn, Texas, attorney also named Jim.

The elder Swarts wrote back to Brown, thanking him for the letter, "which was splendid in its detail, but also your friendship for our boy who has gone on ahead...(W)ho knows, but God, what is best and He has spoken and I am ready to accept his wisdom, though the purpose is not plain."

Brown had to wait more than three months after Exercise Tiger to write Swarts' father and Ken's wife and son because of the military prohibition on recounting what happened. Brown, in his letter, blamed the delay on "pending operations" and was purposely vague on many of the details of that night.

But Nigel Lewis in *Exercise Tiger* was more to the point: "An army that hoped in a few weeks time to take an enemy-held, heavily fortified coastline did not wish it to be known that it had suffered heavy losses in an exercise in 'friendly' coastal waters."

Survivors of heavy combat, Lewis wrote, often received thirty days leave in the states. "But what they got was house arrest. They were told to stay mum."

An April 29, 1944 memo sent by the chief of staff to one of the commanding officers of Brown's unit wrote: "Regarding enemy activity of night 27-28 April during the exercise, members of this command will not mention the incident to military personnel not participating in the exercise nor to civilians either orally or in writing until authorized by this headquarters. Advise all concerned. By command of Major General Collins.

## PAYCHECKS LOST IN BATTLE

In fact, according to the book, Brown and his *507* mates received their monthly pay late because their checks were on the ship, which lay at the bottom of Lyme Bay, more than 160 feet beneath the surface.

By D-Day, Brown had been reassigned as a gunnery officer to a mine sweeper, the USS Staff, and was on the water at Utah Beach when the invasion started. The Staff was one of the lead mine-sweepers for the battle, cruising toward the shore shortly after midnight as Allied aircraft flew overhead to drop bombs on the dug-in Germans. As the ship continued steaming in, gliders and planes carrying paratroopers replaced the bombers.

Then the Naval bombardment started, with massive cannons from battleships, such as the USS Nevada firing at the Germans.

Like the rest of the invading forces, the Staff sliced through five to six feet waves and high tailwinds driving it toward the beach. While far from ideal, the landing went ahead because June 6 was one of only three days that month with a tide low enough to allow the soldiers and their equipment to wade ashore.

Jerry Brown Sr., (left) with survivors of the Exercise Tiger tragedy the day after their ship, the LST 507, was sunk by the Germans. They wore borrowed clothes because their uniforms were ruined after bobbing in the English Channel for hours awaiting rescue.

Scant information was released in the immediate aftermath of Exercise Tiger, especially about the heavy loss of life. It wasn't until the 1980s, when records were being declassified, that word began to spread. To this day, there are few memorials marking the event, although a Sherman tank, lost during maneuvers prior to Exercise Tiger, was pulled from Lyme Bay, near Slapton Sands, in 1984. It now sits on a seaside pedestal in Devon as a reminder of the men lost during Exercise Tiger.

## TIGER DEATH TOLL SURPASSES UTAH BEACH'S

Little more than six weeks after Exercise Tiger, the Allies would storm Normandy the morning of June 6, 1944. The worst action of the five landing zones was at Omaha Beach, where nearly 2,400 men were killed, wounded or missing. At Utah Beach, about ten10 miles west of Omaha, the soldiers came ashore to light resistance, in part because they landed about a mile further west than anticipated due to the ocean currents. Fewer than 200 men were killed, not even a third of the casualties recorded during Exercise Tiger.

By D-Day, Brown had been reassigned as a gunnery officer to a mine sweeper, the *USS Staff*, and was on the water at Utah Beach when the invasion started. The *Staff* was a lead mine-sweeper for the battle, cruising toward the shore while battleships with 305-millimeter cannons fired deadly shells at the Germans.

During the fighting, the *Staff* steamed to the aid of the destroyer *Glennon*, which had struck a mine, and run aground. The *Staff* tried, but failed, to tow the *Glennon* to safety. Instead, most of the *Glennon's* crew — many seriously injured — were taken aboard the *Staff.* The *Staff* Captain, Lt. J.H. Napier, was awarded a Bronze Star medal for saving the lives of the *Glennon* crew.

Another ship, the destroyer escort *USS Rich*, hit a mine while trying to refloat the *Glennon*. The *Rich* sank within fifteen minutes of the explosion, a fifty-foot section of her stern torn apart.

The Normandy invasion was the major turning point in freeing France and the rest of Europe from Nazi control. Once the Allies established that tenuous foothold on the tip of France, the German Army was slowly and inexorably on the retreat, although tens of thousands of lives would still be lost.

When the sun finally set on June 6, roughly 156,000 Allied troops were spread along Normandy's beaches. Close to 4,000 troops died. Five days later, the Allies not only had control of the beaches, but they were moving 50,000 vehicles and some 326,000 troops inland.

Germany, as a result, had to fight on three fronts, with the Russians to the East and the Americans, British, Canadians and others to the West and also in Italy. That made it impossible for Hitler to shift troops from one front to shore up another without weakening his forces.

The French port of Cherbourg was the first objective to be captured by the Allies, on June 26, triggering the Germans retreat in earnest. The port city of Marseille in southern France was another primary target of the Allies. The attack began on August 12 and ended two weeks later. In the days that followed, the *Staff* crew and Ensign Brown went ashore, joyously greeted — as were all the Allies — as liberators by surviving citizens. At one point, Brown was the highest ranking officer in the city, prompting him to joke that he was the mayor of Marseille for a day.

Paris was freed almost simultaneously with Marseille. On May 8, 1945, Nazi Germany surrendered.

Brown stayed with the *Staff* until April of 1945, when he was transferred to another minesweeper, the *USS Deft*. In addition to his gunnery officer duties, he was put in charge of benefits and insurance for the *Deft* crew, records show.

The *Deft* was launched in March of 1943 out of Tampa,

courtesy of the Tampa Shipbuilding Co. Assigned originally to the Mediterranean, the *Deft* assisted in the Allied invasion of France, then was sent to Pearl Harbor in March, 1945, where Brown caught up with her. She was there for maintenance, followed by submarine exercises, according to Navy documents.

## EN ROUTE TO JAPAN AS ATOM BOMB DROPPED

From Pearl Harbor, the *Deft* sailed to Saipan and Okinawa as the Allied forces turned their full attention to Japan. The Allies demanded that Imperial Japan unconditionally surrender on July 26, 1945, threatening "prompt and utter destruction" if the country did not give up the fight.

Of course, it was not an idle threat. The ultra-secret Manhattan Project had created the atomic bomb, the most prolific weapon of mass destruction ever known to man. The Japanese continued fighting, leaving President Harry Truman and the Allies the choice of invading Japan — at an almost unimaginable loss of life to both sides — or dropping the bomb.

So, while the *Deft* and Ensign Brown were sailing toward Japan, President Truman consulted with the British, received their approval, and made the call. Hiroshima and Nagasaki were bombed on August 6 and 9, 1945, killing at least 129,000 people, most of them civilians. *Little Boy* and *Fat Man*, which fell on Hiroshima and Nagasaki, respectively, were the sole nuclear weapons used in war.

The *Deft* arrived at Sasebo, Japan – just north of Nagasaki – about six weeks after the bombs were dropped. She swept mines off the coast of Honshu and served in various occupation duties. Brown told family and friends that clearing mines out of Japanese waters was probably the scariest duty he handled, adding that few sailors wanted to pull up the nets snaring the mines for fear they would explode. He had seen just how destructive a mine could be when it struck a vulnerable part of the ship, undoubtedly recalling how the destroyer *Rich* went down off Normandy in just fifteen minutes. In all, ninety one sailors on the *Rich* were killed or died of wounds following their rescue.

By mid-December of 1945, the *Deft* left for the West Coast of the United States. On February, 28, 1946, Ensign Brown was granted an honorable discharge from the Navy, though he would remain on inactive reserve until August, 1955.

The two minesweepers that Brown served on were turned into scrap long ago. The *Deft* was sold to the Republic of China in 1948 and salvaged for parts and metal in January 1959. The *Staff* was purchased by Southern Scrap Metals Co. of New Orleans, Louisiana in November 1967.

Like many young veterans, Brown received a proclamation signed by President Harry S. Truman upon leaving the service. It read: "To you who answered the call of your country and served in its Armed Forces to bring about the total defeat of the enemy, I extend the heartfelt thanks of a grateful Nation. As one of the Nation's finest, you undertook the most severe task one can be called upon to perform. Because you demonstrated the fortitude, resourcefulness and calm judgment necessary to carry out that task, we now look to you for leadership and example in further exalting our country in peace."

## A KNOCK ON THE DOOR

Decades after the war ended, possibly in 1986 or 1987, Brown and his family was living on the golf course at Orlando Country Club, though his oldest daughters already headed off to college. His wife Caroline answered a knock on the door. It was an older man she had never met before.

"Can I help you?" she asked.

"Does Ensign Brown live here?" he said.

"Well, yes, but he's not in the Navy anymore," she replied.

"Could I speak with him, please?"

"He's at work right now.'

"Could I wait for him?"

Caroline, who told the story to SuSu, ushered him in the house. He quietly waited, while Caroline called her husband and explained what was going on. "He sat at full attention," SuSu said her mother recounted. "He really didn't want to talk. He just sat there and waited and waited."

Brown returned home, but did not recognize the man, who instantly stood up and saluted. "I just wanted to thank you," the man said, "for saving my life."

The two talked and it turned out that Brown had given his life preserver to the man as the LST 507 was sinking in the English Channel during the early morning hours of April 28, 1944. Like Brown and the late ship Capt. James Swarts, they were on the bow of the listing ship. The soldier was holding onto a rail, virtually paralyzed as he stared at the churning water.

"What's the matter, soldier?" Brown asked him.

"I can't swim, sir," was the anguished reply.

Brown took off his jacket and put it on the soldier. "I'm from Florida," Brown said. "I'm a good swimmer. But you've got to go now."

The soldier jumped in and Brown never saw him again — until the surprise visit to Florida that came some three and a half decades after the Exercise Tiger records were declassified.

## ANOTHER BROWN FLIES FOR U.S. TROOPS

Brown's older sister, Texana, also served during the war. She was a pilot in the Women's Air Service and Civil Air Patrol, often flying over the Gulf of Mexico looking for German submarines. In 2010, 66 years after she left the service, she was awarded a Congressional Gold Medal for her efforts.

Tex, whose name was an amalgam of her two grandmothers, Texana and Amanda, graduated in three years from what is now Florida State University, but what was then the Florida College for Women. She earned a degree in economics and accounting and learned to fly as something of a whim.

At the time, she had three roommates and was working at the University of Florida as a secretary. The quartet loved going to Daytona Beach, but had to take a bus because of war restrictions on the use of gasoline. Then, she learned of a company that was offering women free flying lessons. She signed up and became a pilot, according to a 2010 interview she gave to the capgoldmedal.com website for Civil Air Patrol, U.S. Air Force Auxiliary.

The group joined a flying club for $25 a month and Tex became an expert, licensed pilot. That led to her joining the

Civil Air Patrol (CAP) squadron in Sarasota, which included a job as a bookkeeper.

At the start of World War II, only 3.5 percent of licensed pilots in the U.S. were women. They flocked to the CAP and, by the war's end, women made up 20 percent of the program's senior and cadet membership.

While in the service, Tex met her husband, John Meachem, who was a navigator in the Air Force wing of the U.S. Army, said Lucinda Sutton, the middle of three daughters the couple had. After the war, Tex became a school librarian, while Meachem became a salesman and high school math teacher.

John Meachem died in 1991 of a heart attack, prompting Brown to take over his sister's finances. Together with Brown, she had partial ownership of a five-acre citrus plot called the Triangle Grove. It sat near Florida's Turnpike and State Road 50.

Money was tight for Tex, Sutton said, and her brother would give her money, saying it was her share of the Triangle Grove, which Brown, Sr. originally bought for his mother. She, in turn, bequeathed it to him and his sister. Sutton doubted the grove generated that much money. "He was helping her out, but he left her pride intact," Sutton said.

One of the highlights of Tex's later years was an April 2010 ceremony in Fort Lauderdale — she was living in an assisted-living facility nearby — honoring her service. She even got to briefly take over the controls during a nearly hour-long flight in a vintage World War II plane.

"Honest to Pete, I'm really overwhelmed," she said in a video of the event put together by the *Miami Herald*. It has been viewed nearly 10,000 times.

She also was honored in 2007 by the city of Winter Garden with a bronze plaque at the Fowler Groves shopping complex, commemorating her war service.

Texana "Tex" Brown was honored in 2007 by the city of Winter Garden with a bronze plaque at the Fowler Groves shopping complex, commemorating her war service.

Tex, who died quietly in her sleep in 2012, offered this bit of wisdom during her interview to capgoldmedal.com: "I would give women of today the same advice my mother gave me. She told me all my life I could do anything I wanted to do. You just have to work for it. Nobody's going to just give it to you. But in addition to that, you've just got to be bold and push on."

File No.

**U. S. S. STAFF (AM-114)**
Care of Fleet Post Office
New York, N. Y.

July 30, 1944

Dear Dottie and "Donnie,"

I have tried on numerous occasions
to get permission from higher authorities to write this letter, but
as yet haven't. I have thought of both of
you quite often since that tragic night. I
think it is needless to say that ~~the chief~~ Ken
was my best friend aboard.

We arrived in the United Kingdom at Roseneath,
Scotland. From there we went to Falmouth,
England which is located on the southwest tip (?)
of England. We stayed here doing minor maneuvers.
On the 24th we proceeded to a destination I can not
disclose to load army personel and equipment.
After this was completed we started out on the
maneuver. At about 0125 on the morning of the
28th we were attacked by shell fire and at 0210 ~~we~~
~~were hit by the torpedo.~~ This happened about 18 miles out from
Portland, England

I didn't see the ~~chief~~ Ken" after we were
hit but I do know that he was not
wounded and got off the ship without
injury. His death was caused by exposure. (over)

File No.

**U. S. S. STAFF (AM-114)**
Care of Fleet Post Office
New York, N. Y.

July 30, 1944

Dear Dottie and Donnie,

I have tried on numerous occasions to get permission ^from higher authorities to write this letter, but as yet haven't. I have thought of both of you quite often since that tragic night. I think it is needless to say that ~~the thing~~ Ken was my best friend aboard.

We arrived in the United Kingdom at Roseneath, Scotland. From there we went to Falmouth, England which is located on the southwest tip of England. We stayed here doing minor maneuvers(?) On the 24th we proceeded to a destination I can not ~~mention~~ that ~~we~~ load army personel and equipment ~~we held on~~ ~~Tied out on the~~ ~~our army ships~~ May 1, by

File No.

**U. S. S. STAFF (AM-114)**
Care of Fleet Post Office
New York, N. Y.

Dorthy if there is anything I can possibly do to help, please call on me.

Sincerely,
A. F. Brown

File No.

**U. S. S. STAFF (AM-114)**
Care of Fleet Post Office
New York, N. Y.

July 30, 1944

Dear Dottie and Donnie,

I have tried on numerous occasions
to get permission ^from higher authorities to write this letter, but
as yet haven't. I have thought of both of
you quite often since that tragic night. I
think it is needless to say that ~~the they~~ Ken
was my best friend aboard.

We arrive . . .

File No.

**U. S. S. STAFF (AM-114)**
Care of Fleet Post Office
New York, N. Y.

At about 0125 on the morning
of the 28th we were attacked by
shell fire and at 0210 hit by
the torpedo. This happened about 18
miles out from Portland, England.
At the time we were hit we were
with a convoy. Our ship was not
the only one hit. The personel loss
was extremely high

I did not ~~see~~ Ken after we
were hit, but I do know that
. . . wounded and got

File No.

U. S. S. STAFF (AM-114)
Care of Fleet Post Office
New York, N. Y.

At about 0125 on the morning
of the 28th we were attacked by
shell fire and at 0210 hit by
the torpedo. This happened about 18
miles out from Portland, England.
At the time we were hit we were
with a convoy. Our ship was not
the only one hit. The personel loss
was extremely high

I did not see Ken after we
were hit, but I do know that
he was not wounded and got
off the ship without injury. His
death was caused by exposure. I
can assure you that it is not
an unpleasant death. At first you
are cold, but from then on you
became use to it and the end is
like going to sleep. The few of us
that were saved were extremely lucky.
It was very dark that ni

# 4

# NO RETURN TICKET

## GAINING A GLOBAL PERSPECTIVE

The year was 1980 and Gator Brown was in Sydney, Australia in the Southwest Pacific Ocean. He had spent the previous month 600 miles away from Sydney, marveling at New Zealand's natural splendor, from its mountain peaks to its wide range of animal, fungal, and plant life. Traveling the world for the better part of two years, Gator had paused his wandering for a few moments to consider a job offer.

He and his buddy, Craig Karst of Orlando, were thinking hard about becoming cowboys in the Australian Outback. Since they already were in the Southern Hemisphere and only 1,600 miles from the immense, lightly populated interior of Australia, Gator and Karst were eager to try on a new lifestyle. "I'd always wanted to be a cowboy," Gator said.

The main catch was the job called for what could be as much as a six-month commitment. Gator thought he should run the idea past his father, who was back home in Orlando some 8,000 miles away, trying to keep the struggling family business viable.

"I want to see what it's like," Gator told his dad on the long-distance call made from inside an old, rusty phone booth.

The line crackling with static, Brown Sr., replied, "You know, son, you've smelled those roses long enough. Maybe you should just stay there." Then he hung up, the line going dead.

That was not the response Gator expected or was hoping to hear. Two years after graduating from the University of Florida, Gator was twenty five years old, sans a serious girlfriend, without any debt or major possessions and as close to carefree as a young man could be. Virtually all he owned could fit in the backpack slung on his left shoulder.

Like Karst, he was living a vagabond dream and he did not want to give it up. And, although he did not know it then, he also was blazing a path his younger brother Tom would follow within a couple of years.

"It was the most formative time of my life," Gator recalled.

## CASHING IN THE TICKET HOME

His adventure with Karst started in 1978 with a round-trip ticket to and from Heathrow Airport in London. It was a graduation present from Gator's mom and dad. The initial plan was for Gator and Karst — also a recent UF grad — to see a bit of Europe for a few weeks, soak up some culture, knock back a few pints, maybe meet a girl or two, have a lot of fun. Then they would head back to Orlando and the real world, Gator to join his dad's company, Florida Food Products, Karst to work with his dad in the family grove maintenance and citrus business.

But Gator and Karst, whose father was a good friend of Brown Sr., had developed a more evolved vision for their trip. Unbeknownst to their parents, they were going to take off and — who knew? — maybe never come back. They envisioned living out their days surfing off some remote Pacific island, or becoming ski bums in the Alps or finding the true meaning of life with a holy man in India. They really weren't sure where they were headed. They just knew that they were going somewhere far away from their homes in provincial, old Central Florida.

What was the point, after all, of being in the United States? Inflation was high, at 10 percent annually. Jobs not involving parents weren't easy to come by, unless you wanted to park cars or handle crowd control at Walt Disney World. Jimmy Carter was the president and people still weren't sure what to make of him, what with his fifty-five miles per hour federal highway speed limit and encouraging people to wear sweaters to keep their thermostats down during the winter. Europe had economic woes of its own, including a stagnant economy, but come on, it had to be better than Orlando, right?

So, Gator and Karst had worked for a couple of months after graduation, saving up money for their grand adventure. They made one big investment in advance, each purchasing a three-month pass on what is now called Eurail, ensuring they could go anywhere in Europe that the continent-wide system of trains went.

Karst remembered touching down in Heathrow and seeing a huge billboard listing arrivals and departures to and from exotic cities like Lisbon, Barcelona, Amsterdam, Cologne, Berlin and Paris. He shook his head, not quite believing what he was seeing. "There's a whole other world out there," he thought.

The first thing Gator did after landing in London was cash in the return portion of his airline ticket, which is illegal now, but was a fairly common practice then. That gave Gator a few extra British pounds in his wallet. That was important because one pound was equal to nearly two American dollars then. Their extra clothes and assorted odds and ends stuffed into backpacks, Gator and Karst took off for sights and wonders unknown.

## TWENTY EIGHT COUNTRIES IN TWO YEARS

They would see twenty-eight countries, stretching from Europe to the Far East to the Arctic Circle to Australia. They traveled by train, motorcycle, on foot and by hitchhiking. They worked some, too, doing a six-month stretch in the St. Moritz Valley, Switzerland, working ski lifts, and six weeks tying rebar steel rods together for an office tower foundation in Munich.

One of their most important lessons was learning how to stretch their money, living on five dollars to ten dollars a day, staying in rooms and youth hostels that cost as little as one dollar night, even sleeping on top of a train rolling through India. "We were cheap, cheap, cheap," Gator said.

Once, they saved up enough money to buy a couple of used Yamaha motorcycles to help them get around, hopscotching from one country to the next, much like Americans drive from one state to the next, Florida to Georgia to Tennessee. They wanted to ride from Germany — where they bought the bikes — into Israel. Working their way south to Spain, they caught a boat across the Mediterranean Sea into Morocco, then made their way east into Egypt. But they were stopped at the Sinai because of negotiations that eventually became known as the Camp David Accords between Egyptian President Anwar Sadat and Israeli President Menachem Begin. The agreement was orchestrated by President Carter.

Their time abroad overlapped the outgoing administration of Carter and the incoming one of Ronald Reagan, as well as a turbulent era of high inflation and flat business expectations. The Iranian hostage crisis was the big political story. More than fifty American diplomats and citizens were held hostage for 444 days by a group of radical Iranian college students. They were in support of a revolution that toppled the U.S.-backed Shah of Iran from power and led to the religious cabal that still controls the country. The hostages were imprisoned from November 4, 1979 to January 20, 1981, before finally being released.

But politics were not on the minds of Gator and Karst, though they were busy with their own form of diplomacy – making friends with dozens and dozens of other young people who were seeing the world. Karst said he and Gator compiled a black book of names and addresses of friends they made along the way. Periodically, they would call on them and stay a few days if they passed through their village or town.

"We learned how to make the best of things. We learned how to rough it. They were such magnificent surroundings," Karst said.

Once Gator and Karst got split up in a train station in the Netherlands by accidentally boarding two different trains. Since this was long before cell phones and instant and continual communication, they went their separate ways for two weeks. Gator ended up in the Arctic Circle, while Karst went into northern Germany. They reconnected in an Oslo station thanks to a series of letters and calls back home to their respective families.

## DWINDLING RESOURCES

Their Eurail passes ran out at the end of the summer, leaving them without cheap transit. Even worse, they were running low on cash. Karst remembers them having about twenty dollars each. They were in Austria at the time and decided to hitchhike to Munich, where some English friends had found construction jobs doing foundation work on an office tower. They invited Gator and Karst to join them. The pair was hired after telling their employers they were British citizens, too. Although there was no such thing as the European Union back then, a reciprocal agreement was in place allowing citizens of Great Britain and Europe to work in countries other than their own without having to apply for and receive the approval of the local government.

The job lasted six weeks before they were fired after their boss discovered they actually were Americans. Gator and Karst were not too upset because they had replenished their funds. "We made great money," Karst said.

But they were not done working. Prior to going to Munich, they had interviewed with the manager of a ski resort in St.

Moritz. He offered them a job as migrant laborers in an arrangement similar to what happens now in the United States, where foreigners can take jobs Americans are unwilling to fill.

Gator was tasked with helping skiers get attached to T-lines that ferried them up the slopes while remaining on their skis. Karst was in charge of a gondola that held up to eighty people and also ferried them up the mountain. They became adept skiers because they had the slopes to themselves when the resort closed for the day.

At night, the two slept in the equivalent of a dorm room. Between their single beds, Karst said, they affixed a map of the world. They would look at it and talk about where they would go next when their job ended with resort closing for the spring.

Their overriding mantra: "Plan the next day and have fun," Karst said.

## ASIA AND PARADISE

Eventually, they made their way to southern Asia and India, where they rode the trains and stayed on the roof during a trip to Calcutta because it was cooler than being in the stifling heat of the rail cars. They even fell asleep. "There were so many people up there. They were everywhere. You couldn't fall off if you wanted to," Gator said.

They made an extra twenty dollars in the area by smuggling four bottles of gin from neighboring Nepal into India. "We thought we were rich," Gator said. Looking back, Gator said the additional money was hardly worth the angst of the transaction. The India-Nepal border is open, allowing natives of either country to cross freely without passports or visas.

Gator especially enjoyed Koh Samui in southern Thailand. It is a little island filled with waterfalls and rivers and accessible only by ferry. People slept in small huts on the beach and often drank a coconut-alcoholic concoction called a toddy. Gator called the arrangement paradise. "You're having the time of your life," he said, remembering that they often would form a circle on the beach to watch fights between two bulls butting heads.

Gator spent a month during the Christmas holiday of 1979 on the island of Ko Samui, off the east coast of Thailand.

New Zealand ended up being one of his favorite places, Gator said, because of its beauty and "the people are so friendly."

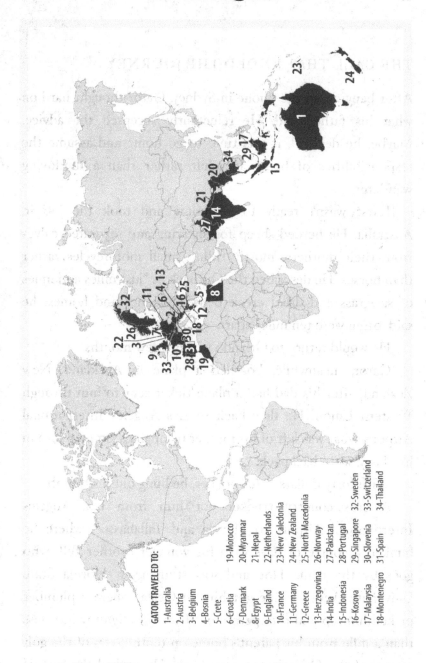

GATOR TRAVELED TO:
1-Australia
2-Austria
3-Belgium
4-Bosnia
5-Crete
6-Croatia
7-Denmark
8-Egypt
9-England
10-France
11-Germany
12-Greece
13-Herzegovina
14-India
15-Indonesia
16-Kosova
17-Malaysia
18-Montenegro
19-Morocco
20-Myanmar
21-Nepal
22-Netherlands
23-New Caledonia
24-New Zealand
25-North Macedonia
26-Norway
27-Pakistan
28-Portugal
29-Singapore
30-Slovenia
31-Spain
32-Sweden
33-Switzerland
34-Thailand

# THE CALL THAT ENDED THE JOURNEY

After hanging up the phone in Sydney, Gator thought hard on what his father said. He reluctantly accepted the advice. Maybe, he decided, it was time to go home and assume the responsibilities of being an adult rather than a fun-loving wanderer.

Karst wasn't ready to go home and took the job in Australia. He herded sheep for shearing and separated calves from their mothers, mostly riding small motorcycles rather than horses. He described the Outback as "just miles and miles of sawgrass and dried creek beds." Ranches and homes, he said, often were ten miles apart.

He would return to Orlando within a few months.

Gator, meanwhile, boarded a plane in Auckland, New Zealand, after his dad had a plane ticket sent to him through Western Union. He flew back to Los Angeles International Airport, what was left of his meager belongings jammed into in his dusty, worn backpack.

With forty dollars in his pocket, he hung out his thumb.

A cross-country trucker got him from Los Angeles International Airport to Florida and Tallahassee, where he bunked a couple of days with his younger brother Bill, who goes by the name Hoe and was studying at Florida State University. Another ride got him to Ocala, where a plumber picked him up and dropped him off on US Highway 441, less than a mile from his parent's home on tenth green of the golf course of the Orlando Country Club. He walked the rest of the way.

It was early evening when he crossed the fairway and saw his parents sitting on the patio, having their usual evening drinks, an Early Times bourbon for his dad and white wine for his mother. She spotted Gator first and let out a surprised yelp.

Gator broke into a smile, as did his dad. His mother started crying. They all hugged. "It was pretty emotional," Gator said.

They had a lot to catch up on. And Gator had accumulated a lifetime of memories in two years that were, in retrospect, "the most formative thing in my life. I learned about people. We're all the same. Everybody wants the same thing, to be loved, to have a family."

His exposure to different cultures would prove beneficial at FFP because their sales typically were greater overseas than in the United States and he could relate to people who had different skin colors and religious and political beliefs. He'd even learned to overcome language barriers. And all those skills would come into play during the coming decades.

⚘

## TOM BROWN EMBARKS ON GLOBAL ADVENTURE

Tom graduated from Bishop Moore High School in 1978, earning varsity letters in soccer and golf. Four years later, he graduated from Florida State University, including spending one semester abroad in Florence. His majored in finance.

After leaving Tallahassee at the age of twenty two, Tom set off for Europe. Using the roundtrip ticket bestowed upon him for graduation by his mom and dad, he was following in the footsteps of his two older brothers, Gator and Bill, or Hoe, both of whom had gone abroad after completing school. Unlike Gator and Tom, Hoe's stay overseas was short, measured in weeks rather than months or years.

Tom decided he was going to finance his travels with about $6,000 he had saved from working summer jobs in high school and college, ranging from being a bellman at Orlando hotels to driving a ski boat at Sea World to stacking soda pop in the Puerto Rico warehouse for FFP. He would spend every last dime before heading home.

Of all his part-time jobs before going to Europe, being a bellman at the Marriott Hotel near the tourist corridor of International Drive was the best experience, Tom said. It taught him how to sell himself as a way to receive good tips as he carried bags from the lobby to a customer's room. The skill came in handy for him as the top salesman for thirty-plus years at FFP, where he quickly learned that he had to first sell himself to a client before he could extoll the virtues of his products.

Tom, who did not have a serious girlfriend back in Orlando, visited fifteen countries during his year-long sojourn: New Zealand, Australia, Singapore, Thailand, India, Nepal, Myanmar, China, Russia, South Korea, Japan, Hong Kong, Sweden, Germany and England. Tom's travels were west to east, while Gator's were the opposite.

Like Gator and Karst, he made friends all over the globe. Though he started out solo, he often found himself moving about with several mates at a time. Europeans, as well as Australians, he said, love to travel, so he often fell in with a group of them. "You would just be with them and travel until you went in different directions," said Tom, who rarely crossed paths with another American.

They would stay in cheap motels — three dollars a night — as well as camp in parks, or even throw a sleeping bag on a bus or in a quiet corner of a train station. "I was pretty much on the move the whole time," Tom said. "I rarely stayed more than three or four days anywhere."

Unlike his big brother Gator, Tom worked little, though he did slow his roaming long enough to harvest mussels in the Nelson Sound in New Zealand and bus tables at a hotel in Queensland, Australia. He also sold his Levis and shirts in Russia because American clothes were hard to get there and people were willing to pay a premium for them. He replaced his rather basic wardrobe with cheap Russian clothes instead.

Tom Brown on a cold morning an Asian mountain range that divides the Indian subcontinent from the Tibetan Plateau.

Tom spent some of his travels with a Dutch woman, Meik Remmers. The pair were detained in China for getting off a train in a town after being told by authorities not to disembark. Wondering what could possibly be the issue, they left the train and took a seat in the station that apparently was off limits to them.

Within moments, he said, they were surrounded by locals, who, it soon became apparent, rarely saw foreigners. Before long, several law enforcement officers wearing green caps with a little red star on the front hustled them into a room. What seemed like a thousand people peered in through the windows, jabbering and pointing at Tom and his friend.

The interrogation was actually funny, Tom said, because neither party could speak the other's language. Eventually, after trying hand signals and slowly enunciating words neither side could understand, the officers gave up and released them.

By then, it was late and Tom and Meik needed a place to spend the night. All they found was a couple of empty beds in the local hospital. In the morning, the pair happily caught the next train out of town.

He was amazed at how poorly the Chinese treated the environment, with dirty, smoke-filled skies from pollution-belching plants to careless littering. While riding on a ship on the Yangtze River, he would watch people eat, then discard their disposable plates or cups into the water. The Yangtze, which stretches almost 4,000 miles, is the longest river in Asia and the third longest in the world. "The environment was just a second thought to them," he said.

## RUSSIA WAS A SAD PLACE

Tom's travels were dominated by talk of former President Ronald Reagan, who was placing missiles in Western Europe as a deterrent to possible expansion by the Soviets — a nation the president often derided as the "Evil Empire." Many Europeans feared the move by the ex-movie-star-turned president would make war more likely, rather than less. "They were pissed," said Tom, who sided with the Europeans. "You get kind of influenced by that."

At the time, the USSR still controlled most of Eastern

Europe, though small cracks were forming. Soviet leader Mikhail Gorbachev tried to quell a Democratic push by countries under Soviet control by offering small economic concessions, but the Communist Party lost its grip in November 1989, when the Berlin wall came down. It had been built after World War II to keep East Germans from defecting to the West. Once the wall fell, much of Eastern Europe broke away from Russia.

Tom actually spent time in Russia, which, at that time, was slowly opening its doors to foreigners, much like China was doing. He described Russia "as a sad place, grey. People wouldn't talk to you. Of course they weren't really allowed to."

One highlight for him was riding on the Trans-Siberian Railway, which connects Moscow with the Far East. Stretching some 5,772 miles, it is the longest railway line in the world, spanning eight time zones and taking eight days to complete. Foreigners, Tom said, were all seated in one car, though they were free to walk into other cars. Much of the trip, he said, was through the long, monotonous grasslands of Mongolia and Siberia, passing countless yurts, or portable, round tents favored by the Mongols.

By the fall of 1983, Tom was ready to come home. Unlike Gator, he did not need his father to tell him that the time of fun and games had come to an end. With his wallet becoming thinner by the day, Tom wanted to start making money and needed no encouragement to return. In retrospect, Tom said, Nepal was his favorite stop because of the majestic mountains. He even slept in huts there, sometimes gazing at the pollution-free, star-filled sky, picking out various constellations.

Tom Brown's post-grad travels educated him about
international customs.

Like Gator, Tom was broke when he decided to head home
and had to ask his dad to forward him a ticket to fly him back.
Tom left out of Heathrow in London.

Tom's biggest takeaway from his year away was that he
came to understand different points of view by seeing the
world not just through American eyes, but also those of Europeans or Asians or even Russians. "You learn," he said, "how to
interact with other cultures."

That experience was crucial for him at FFP because much
of their sales were overseas, especially in Korea and Japan. "I
had a leg up," he said. "So many Americans go to Japan and
they look like lost puppies. They couldn't assimilate."

**TOM TRAVELED TO:**

1-Australia
2-Bangladesh
3-Burma
4-China
5-England
6-Finland
7-Germany
8-Hong Kong
9-India
10-Malaysia

11-Mongolia
12-Nepal
13-Netherlands
14-New Zealand
15-Russia
16-Singapore
17-Sweden
18-Thailand
19-United States

## THE BACKBONE

### THE BROWNS, PETERSES AND PEOPLE OF COLOR

The Brown and Peters families employed hundreds of African Americans for domestic, citrus and sugarcane duties and other chores and projects dating as far back as the 1920s. But three people of color became more than just employees and spent virtually their entire working lives with the broods before and after the marriage of Jerry Brown and Caroline Peters.

In some ways, the Brown/Peters relationship with blacks they hired and often befriended was a reflection of the times in Florida and the Deep South. Due to Jim Crow laws, segregation of the races and outright racism stretching back to the Civil War and beyond, economic opportunities for blacks were severely limited through much of the twentieth century, especially during the first seven decades. Blacks could reliably find work involving manual labor and housekeeping, but frequently were denied a quality education and shut out of more lucrative jobs and professions.

A trio of African Americans — Arthur Faircloth, Willie Sager and Barbara Lampkin — each worked at least forty years for the Browns and Peters. Faircloth and Sager, both deceased, spent time in the groves, performed handyman duties and ran errands. Lampkin cleaned.

The three transcended the usual employer-employee connection with the Browns and Peterses to one of mutual affection and respect, Gator, Tom, Brenda, SuSu and Lampkin recalled. "They were a fixture, a part of the family," Gator said.

The Browns often gave clothes they outgrew to Lampkin, Sager and Faircloth to share with their families, Gator said. Brown Sr., Gator recalled, gave a used pickup truck to Sager, who over the years became a trusted confidant to his employer.

"They were good to us and we tried to return the favor," Gator said.

Jerry and Caroline Brown, born and raised in Florida, were well aware of the racial dynamics and segregation of the era, Gator and Tom said. It was impossible not to see it in play every day. But they did not approve, Gator said. "They knew what was going on," Gator said of his parents. "They weren't a part of it."

They never spoke in derogatory terms to — or about — their African American workers or treated them differently than white employees, Gator and Tom said. They were told as youngsters, both said, to mind Faircloth, Sager and Lampkin just as much as their own parents.

Faircloth, in fact, became Tom's and Gator's first boss. As teens, Tom and Gator often were sent by their father into the groves around the Peterses' old homestead to weed and prune, with Faircloth overseeing the work.

"He would put a hoe in your hand and make you hoe around a bit," said Gator, who added that Faircloth was almost too nice to the young Brown boys and rarely pushed them to work very hard, even though they were in trouble with their parents and the grove work was supposed to be punishment.

## EVER PRESENT – BARBARA LAMPKIN

Lampkin was hired by the Browns in 1961 before retiring during the early 2000s because of arthritic pain. She spent two days a week — every Monday and Wednesday — with the Browns and cleaned for other families in the Country Club of Orlando neighborhood as well.

"I was working hard, doing everything," said Lampkin, seventy-four, who attributes the arthritis in her hands and knees to the strenuous labor she performed. Her duties included ironing, scrubbing floors, changing the beds, polishing silver, serving drinks and food at parties – basically just about every household chore but cooking.

The Browns, Lampkin said, "were sweet people, really nice people" who treated her well. "They were kind to me. I don't really have any complaints about them," said Lampkin, who still lives about fifteen minutes away by car from the Browns old Country Club residence in a largely black community known as Little Egypt.

Other whites, whom she declined to name, often were dismissive of her, Lampkin said, particularly when she worked social gatherings at the Brown home. "They just walked by me, would say nothing," she recalled. "Some weren't too friendly." She would not elaborate, her reluctance to speak not uncommon for blacks who performed domestic chores back then.

Through the decades, Lampkin said, she grew close to Caroline Brown, becoming her friend as much as her house-keeper. Caroline asked Lampkin to spend time with her during her final weeks, when she was bedridden with the brain cancer that took her life in 2007. Lampkin was in the room with SuSu and Brenda when Caroline died.

"She trusted me so much," Lampkin said. "She liked me so much. She just wanted me there.

She was a brave, brave lady. She told everybody she had lived a good life and was ready to go."

Lampkin said the ties she and Caroline shared were such that words often were unnecessary, though they would make small talk to while away the hours. "We just talked about different things," said Lampkin, who spent much of her time in a recliner in Caroline's bedroom. "I can't hardly remember."

Her impression of Jerry Brown Sr., was that he was, "smart, serious, but nice." He usually was at work when she was cleaning the house.

Susie Hupp was Lampkin's first Orlando employer and was a neighbor of the Browns in the Country Club subdivision. She recommended that the Browns hire Lampkin, whose starting pay was one dollar an hour, although she received numerous raises through the years.

Lampkin and Hupp have remained close friends in much the same way as Caroline and Lampkin. Hupp, no longer drives and resides in an assisted living facility, often catches a ride with Lampkin to go shopping.

Originally from Georgia, Lampkin moved to Florida when she was eighteen to be with her father. Lacking a college degree or professional work experience, Lampkin started cleaning houses to earn money.

Orlando was still a segregated community when Lampkin arrived, despite the fact the U.S. Supreme Court had ruled seven years earlier that public schools could not be divided by race. To this day, downtown Orlando has a road called Division Street that for many decades literally marked the line between white neighborhoods on the east and black communities on the west.

A retired *Orlando Sentinel* columnist, Hupp characterized the Browns as a quintessential Southern family, in part because the children all had unusual nicknames: Gator, Hoe (Bill), SuSu, Bop (Brenda) and Boom Boom (Tom). The Browns and children in the neighborhood, including Susie's son Scott, would play games such as baseball and football in a nearby empty lot. The Brown's house, Hupp said, was rarely locked and it seemed as if Faircloth, Sager or Lampkin were always there.

Hupp called Caroline Brown "the nicest, kindest, most loving woman I knew. I still miss her." Caroline, she said, had one quirk: She was reluctant to share her age with others, perhaps because of a touch of vanity or a fear that some might think she was too old to form a lasting friendship.

The Browns, Hupps and several other families raised money for Lampkin when her arthritis became debilitating.

The fund, Lampkin said, was enough to allow her to retire. "Thank you, Jesus," she said of the money.

## UNCOMMON BONDS BETWEEN THE RACES

Long-standing and affectionate bonds between white employers and black employees were not overly common in the Central Florida of yesteryears, but they did occur, according to Dr. Julian Chambliss, a professor of history and English at Michigan State University (MSU). He has extensively studied race relations in the South, Florida and Metro Orlando.

For African Americans, Chambliss said, finding full-time work with people who were good to them was the exception, not the rule. So, he said, they would pragmatically stick around if their employer was kind, rather than rude or worse.

"It was really beneficial to the African American household. It made a lot of sense. Steady labor, steady income," said Chambliss, who taught at Rollins College in Winter Park for eighteen years before switching to MSU in 2018.

Though employer-employee interactions rarely are on equal footing — regardless of race — Chambliss said the emotional attachments between the Browns and the trio of Lampkin, Faircloth and Sager undoubtedly were genuine. "These relationships are real," he said.

Like Lampkin, Faircloth was a good example of an enduring connection. He was hired by Phil C. Peters, Caroline's father, during the 1920s, possibly as early as 1921, after moving south to Winter Garden from Cuthbert, Ga. Along with his wife Ida Mae and daughter Johnny, Faircloth lived in a small house within a ninety-acre tract of citrus groves owned by Peters. The Faircloths' place was less than a stone's throw from the two-story Peters home.

The family relied on longtime workers.

Faircloth would outlive Peters by more than two decades, but Brown fulfilled a promise to his father-in-law that Faircloth would have a job as he long as he lived.

Phil Cudahy, who frequently lived with the Peters during the 1940s as a child and was named after her grandfather, remembered Faircloth as a kind, loving man who would magically appear whenever his name was called. "He would just be there all of a sudden," she said.

Cudahy's father married Caroline's older sister, Frances, after a short courtship as World War II was raging. Then Capt. Tom McGehee flew B-17s in the European Theater during the War, so Frances and her young daughter Phil stayed with the Peterses in the flyer's absence.

Cudahy said her grandmother loved to tell one particular story about her when she was little more than a toddler, maybe three years of age. It was several days before Christmas and young Phil could not keep her hands off the brightly wrapped presents under a decorated fir tree. In fact, she ripped open all the packages. Arthur happened upon little Phil while she was in the act. But instead of putting an end to her antics, he watched in amusement.

"Arthur," Phil Peters asked Faircloth upon discovering little Phil immersed in the boxes and torn wrapping paper. "Why didn't you stop her?"

"I just couldn't, Mr. Phil," Faircloth replied. "She was having so much fun."

Faircloth, who was fond of cigars and was a master barbecuer, often worked in the groves, along with taking care of the Peterses' house and property. He tended to a variety of vegetables and spent hours in a rose garden with Margaret Peters. The two would weed, water and plant side by side, Cudahy said.

He also cared for a patch of sugarcane that grew in the back of the property, closer to Black Lake. Faircloth often would grind the sugarcane into a sweet liquid everyone enjoyed drinking, Cudahy said. The practice almost turned deadly one day when he lost his right arm after it became stuck in the electric grinder. He had used a manual machine for years and likely forgot that the blades of the new model would continue turning once a jammed bit of cane was dislodged.

## FAIRCLOTHS, PETERS KNEW LOYALTIES

During the Great Depression of the 1930s, Peters told Faircloth that citrus prices had fallen so much that he might not be able to pay him, Cudahy said of an account told to her by her mother.

"If you want to work for someone else," Peters said, "I would understand."

"I'm staying right here," Arthur is said to have replied. "I know if you eat, me and my family will eat, too."

Cudahy later became a vocal supporter of civil rights and heckled the late George Wallace, the segregation-backing governor of Alabama, when she was a student at Auburn University. She said the inequality between the races hit her as she grew up. "I was a teenager before I started to get the picture," she said.

But, she said, the Peterses were loyal to the Faircloths — and vice versa. "For their situation," she said of the Faircloths, "it couldn't have been better at that time. They were taken care of."

The Peterses, she said, were as fair as the times allowed. "There was never a derogatory word I heard said," she said. "I had to mind them as equally as I had to mind my family. For me, they were a model and loving people."

After Peters and his wife died, Faircloth and his wife Ida Mae worked for Caroline and Jerry Brown. The black couple continued living at the grove house, near where the Peters had resided. Ida Mae cooked for the Browns, while Faircloth cared for the grove property and structures, as well as going to the Browns' home at the Country Club to lend a hand. As with his former employer Margaret Peters, Faircloth also tended to a flower garden with Caroline Brown. He helped set up a rock garden at the Country Club residence to mimic the one at the Peters' home.

SuSu remembers Faircloth often coming by the house. Everyone called him "Auuthah," stretching out the first part of his name, she said.

Faircloth died Oct. 15, 1986, with services held at the Bethlehem Missionary Baptist Church in Winter Garden, where he was a deacon. His wife preceded him in death. In a picture of his church funeral notice, he is burly, with a cigar in his mouth. He was lauded as "a Christian soldier who lived a life that was well worth being emulated. He was active in all phases of the Church's program. He was known in Winter Garden...as a kind and gentle man, and as one who would share whatever he had with his fellow man. He was respected by everyone who came in contact with him."

## WILLIE SAGER WAS A POWERFUL MAN

Sager worked mostly with Brown Sr., and Ray Gatch, who managed the groves and citrus production for Florida Food Products for close to forty years. The three often seemed inseparable, said Monty Gatch, Ray's son.

The trio all died within about a year of each other: Ray Gatch in his sleep April 28, 1994; Brown Sr., of congestive heart failure May 14, 1995; and Sager of diabetic complications November 7, 1996. Gatch was 66, Brown, 73, and Sager 68.

"He (Sager) was a great, great guy," said Monty Gatch, who as a child would often accompany his father to the groves. That's where Monty met Sager, a large man who weighed in excess of 275 pounds.

Sager, Monty said, would gather up all the empty soda bottles left behind by the pickers. Periodically, Sager would take young Gatch to a Winn Dixie grocery store to trade them in for the five-cent-per-bottle deposit. Sager gave the money to Gatch.

Gator and Tom cannot say with certainty when Sager was hired, but he was with Florida Food Products when they joined the company in 1980 and 1983, respectively. Sager started out in the groves for FFP — possibly during the late 1950s — and would recruit the pickers and other laborers. He handled their pay, too.

Gator and Tom remember Sager as a powerful man capable of picking up a large tractor tire by himself and throwing it into the back of a pickup truck. "He was strong as an ox," Tom said.

That strength was important in the physically demanding work that was typical in a citrus grove. It was customary then for blacks to work in the fields, climbing wooden ladders to twist and pull off the fruit from trees that could reach ten feet or more in height. They placed the oranges in a dirty cotton bag slung across a shoulder.

When the satchel was full, they would dump the oranges into bins that were snatched up by motorized carts equipped with mechanized arms and called goats. They unloaded the oranges onto trailered trucks headed for packing houses or processing plants. Sager started out with the Browns driving a goat.

"The oranges had to be picked. They (African Americans) got the bad end of the deal," Tom said. "It's hot working orange groves in the summer. It's dirty."

Citrus labor was segregated by race, too. Blacks were outside, while whites labored indoors in the plants and packing houses, where the work of sorting good oranges from culls and other tasks was slightly less taxing. Ten-hour days or longer were common during the harvest season for blacks and whites.

"Mutual dependence" was Gator's description of blacks and whites in the citrus industry. Blacks eventually were replaced in the groves with migrants from Mexico. The transition started during the 1960s and largely was complete by the late 1970s, early 1980s.

Until the disastrous freezes of the early 1980s, citrus sprawled across Central Florida and dominated the interior of the state all the way down to massive Lake Okeechobee. Clermont, essentially a residential suburb west of Orlando, used to be covered with groves. The town was famous for its 226-foot tall observation tower that tourists used to climb to marvel at all the citrus trees. Walt Disney is said to have gone to the top of it while scouting out the region for the theme park he would open in 1971, forever changing the landscape and culture of Central Florida. Still in use, the tower view now is almost solely housing developments.

## SAGER WOULD NOT VENTURE INTO OCOEE

Sager, whose father worked in the groves before him, was committed to Brown Sr., and, among his duties, often drove him places. He became close to Gator, through the years, too, giving him a calf to celebrate the birth of his son, Alexander Z, in 1988. The animal stayed at Sager's small ranch in Eustis.

Once, during the 1960s, Sager drove Brown Sr., and a couple of his friends to a Florida Gators football game in Gainesville, Gator said. They stopped at a shop on the way back, with Sager waiting in the car, the engine idling.

A white Florida Highway Patrol trooper pulled up and asked Sager what he was doing sitting in a nice car with the engine running, wasting gas. Sager replied he was waiting for his boss inside the shop. For some reason, the officer did not like the answer and told Sager to move along. Sager refused, saying he could not leave without Brown and his associates. That response upset the officer, who apparently did not like his authority being ignored by a black man. Fortunately, Brown came out and quickly diffused the confrontation, Gator said.

Gatch remembers an outdoor party thrown by his father and Brown Sr., where Sager was grilling the meat over red-hot charcoal. After everyone was seated and eating, Sager made himself plate. At that point, one white man told Sager it was time for him to leave, apparently because his grilling was complete. The elder Gatch and Brown told Sager to stay put and exchanged some unpleasant words with their offensive guest, Monty said.

The Browns were "nice people," who were kind and considerate of Sager, said Evelyn Sager Thomas, Sager's 81-year-old sister. She described her brother as "a wonderful, independent black man. Very good. Very good. And by independent I mean he wouldn't back down."

But one place Sager would not go, even if Brown Sr., requested it, was Ocoee, Gator said. The northwest Orange County town once had a thriving black community, but more than fifty African American residents were killed by marauding whites and Ku Klux Klan members because they tried to vote in November, 1920. One of the leaders of the black community, July Perry, was lynched. Most of the blacks who survived fled the town, never to return.

Census data shows no blacks lived in Ocoee again until 1981. According to local historians, a sign posted at least until 1959 at one of the town limits said, "Dogs and Negroes Not Welcome." Ocoee now boasts more than 46,000 residents, roughly 19 percent of whom are African Americans, the U.S. Census shows.

Chambliss said he was not surprised by Sager's reluctance to go anywhere near Ocoee, even forty to fifty years after the murderous incident. "Can you blame him?" Chambliss asked.

Sager was born and raised in Eustis, one of twenty-three children, said his sister Evelyn Thomas, who lives in Fort Lauderdale. He was a respected member of the black community there, often acting as a liaison with the whites who essentially ran the rural area. "He (Sager) was the go-to guy," said Frank Gaylord, a Eustis attorney and amateur historian.

Gaylord, who specializes in estate planning and probate, started practicing law in Lake County during the early 1970s. He remembers meeting with long-time Lake County Judge Buddy Aulls decades ago when Willie came by. "Under no uncertain terms did I have any priority," Gaylord said. "Willie had the priority."

The judge, Gaylord said, asked him to leave so he could speak privately with Sager. Gaylord thought highly of Sager. "Whatever he said, he did." Gaylord said. "Willie never pulled any punches."

Gaylord's father, Harry, was friends with Brown Sr. Frank Gaylord first met Gator thirty years ago at a Rotary Club gathering and while serving on various civic boards together.

Aulls, who died in 2009 after a fifty-year career in law, apparently made a few traffic tickets disappear for Gator and Tommy — but only at the urging of Sager. Gator said his propensity for speeding eventually caught up with him because Aulls eventually told Sager that he would not forgive any more tickets, Gator said.

Aulls, Gaylord said, "always did what he thought was the right thing."

Race relations in Lake County for many decades "were pretty pitiful," said Gaylord, whose father was an attorney in Eustis starting during the 1930s. Together, the Gaylords ran one of the most prominent firms in the county for decades.

Even though most public schools were integrated by the late 1960s, it was not uncommon to hear Lake County high school bands play a Confederate anthem, "Dixie," at football games. That practice sparked a large-scale fight at a game hosted by Evans High School, which has a largely black student population in west Orlando.

Gaylord's younger brother John was in the high school band and his father implored him and his mates to stop playing "Dixie." They didn't listen and even flew a Confederate flag at the school. Harry Gaylord's request, Frank Gaylord said, led to a call late the next day from the infamous Willis McCall, the late Lake County sheriff and suspected Ku Klux Klan member. McCall was not happy that the elder Gaylord wanted to change Southern traditions at the school, Frank Gaylord said.

"Willis, you must be getting old," Harry Gaylord replied. "I've been waiting for your call since 5 (p.m.)."

## FEW ECONOMIC PROSPECTS IN LAKE COUNTY

Lake County was a poor place, Gaylord said, as was most of Central Florida during much of the twentieth, or at least the first two-thirds of it. That was before Walt Disney World opened, changing the economics of the region and state by ushering in what is now a gaggle of theme parks and tourist attractions collectively worth billions of dollars.

"Back then, there were grove owners, professionals and everybody else," Gaylord said. "It was tough to make a living, no matter what color you were."

The way blacks were treated, he said, "was a matter of the times...History is history."

Evelyn Thomas, a retired certified hospital technician, said growing up black in Lake County was hard, especially with elected officials like McCall wielding immense power. The Lake County sheriff for twenty-eight years, McCall was investigated by state and federal authorities numerous times for civil rights violations and inmate abuse, including murder, but was never convicted.

McCall lost a re-election bid in 1972 after being exonerated in the death of Tommy J. Vickers, a mentally disabled black prisoner who died in his custody. In 2007, the Lake County Commission removed his name from a road named in his honor because he was a "bully lawman whose notorious tenure was marked by charges of racial intolerance, brutality and murder," according to an article in the *Orlando Sentinel*.

Chambliss said the old South ran on a caste system where whites of little means often would employ blacks who had even fewer economic resources. Brown Sr. grew up with a black housekeeper, even though he was twelve when his father died of a heart attack, leaving the family with meager finances. His mother took a clerical position with the Winter Garden Health Department to make ends meet.

Lucinda Sutton, whose mother Tex was Jerry Brown's older sister, said a black woman named Lucy who lived in the so-called quarters (an all-black neighborhood) cooked and washed clothes for the family.

It was a complex relationship, Sutton said. "They knew and loved them and cared about them," Lucinda said of the Browns' attitude towards the African American help. But, Sutton added, "They definitely weren't equal."

# 6

# FROM ORANGES TO SODA
## MAXIMIZING PRODUCTION WAS THE GOAL

Visions of a multimillion-dollar payoff never entered the thoughts of Gator and Tom Brown when they joined Florida Food Products. They were fixated on survival and keeping the company alive because it had fallen hard. Brown Sr., had suffered a series of financial setbacks during the hyper-inflation of the 1970s, plus a heart attack in 1975 that had sapped his stamina. The company, as a result, was at a nadir, going from as many as 400 employees down to a handful.

"Things were really slow," said Charlie Hamrick, who spent nearly forty-five years at FFP before retiring as vice president of operations in 2011. "I was doing just about nothing. Just looking for things to do."

Brown Sr., Hamrick said, was tired and welcomed his sons into the fold, hoping they would bring much-needed energy and new ideas with them. "He was very happy that they came in and revived it," Hamrick said. "It paid off. It really did. I really admire them for that."

FFP's biggest problem was the collapse of the two-pronged strategy it had followed successfully for decades: Processing citrus into concentrate and canning carbonated beverages.

Citrus had been a growing and profitable business from the very start, but cheaper orange concentrate imported from Brazil had been eating away at sales for years. Big-time players like Coca-Cola, Tropicana and Lykes-Pasco were vacuuming up supplies that had been diminished by a series of freezes. Rampant development sparked by a plethora of continually expanding theme parks in the region began gobbling up old groves and turning them into countless tracts of production-assembly houses. The sandy soils so hospitable to oranges were suddenly worth more as homesites than as citrus.

Competition and a major equipment malfunction during the early 1970s had pretty much ended the soda pop segment for FFP, forcing Brown Sr., to sell off all his plants and lease the warehouse space in Eustis, which became a critical revenue stream.

Try as he might, Brown Sr. had not devised a new game plan for FFP. He largely was living off reserves from the good years, plus some smaller income lines, such as a grove-care business and renting warehouse space to the Shasta beverage company. But those streams of money did not come close to replacing citrus and soda pop. Florida Food Products, which had invariably turned a profit, was slowly fading.

It was difficult for Brown Sr., to handle. The numbers just didn't add up the way they used to, no matter how many different ways he punched them into the old-fashioned, hand-cranked adding machine he kept on his desk.

The holder of an accounting degree from the University of Florida, Brown Sr., he had always wanted to be his own boss. He had tried working for others, but was not happy being told what to do. He had worked for the state of Florida for a while, and in sales for several citrus and food companies after being honorably discharged from the Navy in 1946, following the end of World War II.

At one point, he was a sales manager for the Cross & Blackwell food conglomerate, which had offices in West Palm Beach. The company was run by Jack Menzies, who as a lieutenant in the Army had survived the sinking of a ship that Brown served on during the War. No one can say now if Brown and Menzies knew each other while in the service, but the shared experience certainly was fundamental to their relationship. Years later, Cross & Blackwell, Brown processed and sold sour orange concentrate for several years from a dedicated grove in Apopka by State Road 436 and U.S. Highway 441. FFP sold it to Cross & Blackwell, which produced marmalade.

Brown Sr., who had married the former Caroline Peters in 1949, made his first entrepreneurial move in 1953. He bought a citrus packing house in Bartow, in part with $10,000 he borrowed from his father-in-law, Phil C. Peters, a powerful Winter Garden citrus grower who owned about 900 acres, which was a large holding at the time.

A year later, Brown Sr., sold the facility at a profit and bought the Eustis plant from the Golden Gift company with two partners, Hurt Bickerstaff and Bill Hart. They had met and become friends while working for a packing house in Dade

City. The purchase price is uncertain, but it likely was in the range of $150,000, according to Gator and Tom Brown.

The three new owners would not stay together long, though not by choice. Much to the dismay of Brown and Hart, they became the sole owners in 1959, when Bickerstaff died in a mysterious plane crash while flying from Tampa to New Orleans. Tom Brown, born in 1960 and the youngest of the five children brought into the world by Jerry and Caroline Brown, was given the middle name of Hurt, in honor of Bickerstaff.

The plane, a DC-7B, started in Miami, picked up Bickerstaff and others in Tampa, and was supposed to stop in New Orleans, before going on to Los Angeles, according to numerous media reports at that time. Shortly after midnight, the plane dropped off an Air Force radar screen at 14,000 feet, crashing into the Gulf of Mexico. The wreckage was found in ninety feet of water, with all forty two people passengers dead, their bodies scattered about the Gulf.

Investigators could not come up with an official cause for the accident, citing a lack of evidence, according to newspaper reports. There was speculation that a bomb went off inside the plane because pieces of the craft were scattered over a relatively small area and only one of the passengers, reports at the time said, had donned a life preserver. According to Wikipedia, some believe the bomb was planted as part of a life insurance scam. But that theory was never proven.

A grieving Brown Sr., used the company life insurance settlement for Bickerstaff to buy out Hart and become the only owner of FFP.

## BROWN SR. WINS EVAPORATOR GAMBLE

Brown Sr., was not afraid to gamble with his business and, along with Bickerstaff and Hart, made his first big bet in 1957. He won big, first when he bought a used evaporator from an Ocala milk plant — still in use today — that greatly increased the company's ability to process citrus. Later that year, a deep freeze hit the state, dropping temperatures into the twenties, which damaged some of the trees and turned the pulp inside the oranges to mush.

At the time, the U.S. Department of Agriculture (USDA) — which regulated the citrus industry — balked at processing the tainted oranges into concentrate and juice, contending it might not be of high enough quality. But while everyone else let the thawing oranges pile up in their storage bins while they argued with the USDA, Brown Sr. went ahead with processing. "We're making it, we're selling it," Brown Sr., said at the time. "If we don't, we're broke."

The USDA reversed its decision several weeks later, which was a boon for FFP. The company had a head start on everyone else and was able to get its concentrate — now selling at a premium because of the scarcity caused by the freeze — to market first. The exact numbers are no longer available, but FFP profits took flight.

Glenn Tyre, a teenager at the time, remembers the 1957 freeze. Brown Sr., Tyre said, bought up the fruit quickly from his family's small groves in Lake County and anywhere else he could find citrus. They processed it into juice concentrate and stored it in fifty-five-gallon drums. Brown Sr. also bought oranges from Cuba and processed them in Eustis. Cuban citrus provided a redder color, improving the concentrate's color and increasing its value.

"He went and found oranges wherever," said Tyre, who described Brown Sr. as innovative. "He constantly was thinking ahead, trying to stay ahead with projects and inventions."

Tyre, who now sells real estate, said his father did business with Brown Sr., in part because it was a cash transaction. Larger processors and cooperatives would pay the grower at season's end after settling the accounting ledgers, while Brown typically wrote a check within thirty days, if not sooner.

"He was a gentleman," Tyre said of Brown Sr. "He never complained. He just kept going."

Though the new evaporator was small by today's standards, FFP became the tenth-largest processor in the state, just before such behemoths as Tropicana and Minute Maid entered the market. With oranges, FFP pursued independent growers, or those not associated with cooperatives, which were popular then. Over time, more than half of his supply came from the groves of his father-in-law Peters, a legendary

Phil C. Peters promoted Florida citrus and FFP.

grower whose father had settled in Central Florida during the late 1880s and planted and grew orange trees from seed.

Before long, FFP also expanded into industrial freezer storage, citrus pallet/pulp manufacturing for animal feed and orange oil production for the flavor industry. But Brown Sr., also realized the plant had to expand beyond citrus and its related products to run year-round and maximize profits. FFP essentially made soda pop on one side of the plant and processed citrus on the other.

Most citrus processing plants essentially operated during the winter, getting fresh fruit ready for sale up North and taking the blemished oranges, or culls, and turning them into concentrated juice, a process that was developed in 1948. That product had revolutionized the industry, allowing parents across the country to add water to a lump of orange-colored concentrate and have the equivalent of fresh-squeezed juice loaded with vitamin C for the family breakfast every morning.

But Brown Sr., believed the plant was capable of more and he began tinkering with the design of steel cans. In 1958, FFP became the first manufacturer to devise a way to fully seal the lids to the body, preventing the pressurized contents of carbonated beverages from leaking or exploding.

## FFP LANDS COCA-COLA DEAL

Innovation in hand, Brown Sr., contacted a longtime friend, Chapman Root, who bottled Coca-Cola at a plant he owned in Daytona Beach and was one of the largest and most powerful of the Coke bottlers in the country. During the early 1900s, Root's grandfather had founded the Root Glass Company, which designed and patented the iconic wasp-waist Coca-Cola bottles. Chapman Root eventually became chairman of the country's largest Coke bottling company and, in 1982, sold his majority interest in the operation to the parent company of Coca-Cola for $417.5 million, according to media reports.

After talking with Brown Sr., Root signed on. That allowed Root to become the first in the country to sell Coke not only in bottles, but also in cans — which did not have a pull-off tab and required an opener. Before long, FFP became the largest canners of carbonated beverages east of the Mississippi River. At one time, the company owned and operated eight plants: Syracuse, Baltimore, Eustis, Birmingham, Charlotte, Pittsburgh, Cincinnati and Puerto Rico. Along with Coca-Cola, FFP clients included Shasta, Winn Dixie and Kroger.

Jerry Brown Sr. helped pioneer an entire line of canned sodas with plant operations throughout the Eastern U.S. and beyond.

Brown Sr., also made Fresca, a carbonated, grapefruit-flavored drink, and Chug-a-Lug root beer, both his own brands. His spouse, Caroline, came up with the name and the slogan for the root beer, "Snuggle up with Chug-a-Lug." SuBren Packing Co., named after their girls, became the holding company. The couple handed out cans of Chug-a-Lug at their Orlando home to children during Halloween. All told, FFP grew to 400 employees.

In 1964, Brown Sr., and Menzies together would buy 1,200 acres of orange and grapefruit groves in St. Lucie County for $5.5 million. It was the largest citrus grove sale in Florida history at the time, according to an article in the *Orlando Sentinel*. Brown Sr., processed the citrus at the Eustis plant.

Brown Sr., also bought 500 acres of sugarcane near Lake Okeechobee a few years earlier, figuring it would be a cheaper source of sugar than buying it in a refined state for the soda pop part of the business. But he ended up making more money by selling the sugar to co-ops rather than using it himself, especially after President Dwight D. Eisenhower halted all trade with Cuba during October 1960. That boycott included sugar, skyrocketing the price.

The land was long ago sold by Brown Sr., though the family still owns a long, skinny acre that is landlocked and essentially worthless.

By the mid-to-late 1960s, FFP was going strong, pumping out concentrate and soda pop. The Puerto Rico plant became a major hub and Brown Sr., had aspirations of becoming the main supplier of carbonated beverages to the Caribbean and South America.

In a May 4, 1968 interview with the *San Juan Star*, Brown

Sr., said the Puerto Rico plant, near San Juan, was capable of producing 450 cans per minute. Coke was one of the main customers, along with Pepsi-Cola, Seven-Up, Royal Crown Cola, Tru-Ade and Chevy Chase. Brown Sr., developed some in-house beverages, too, including lemon champagne and Kola champagne, which are very sweet and remain popular drinks to this day in Puerto Rico. The plant ran twenty four hours a day with twenty men on the production floor during each of three shifts. Brown Sr., told the paper the annual payroll would be $275,000.

At one point during the 1960s, he owned two helicopters, which he used to spray his citrus groves. He had one land in an open field of their Orlando subdivision to take all the kids for a ride, Gator said. About that time, he also started introducing his children to the family business.

Brenda Holson, a retired pediatrician, worked a couple of summers for her father, keeping the books at the Fairvilla office in Orlando, not far from their new home in the Orlando Country Club subdivision, hard by the tenth fairway of the golf course. She said she was not sure of the intricacies of the business, but she knew how to balance numbers. Once, she said, she found a discrepancy that saved the company $20,000. "You just paid for your summer," Brown Sr., told her.

## OPPORTUNITY KNOCKING

Holson remembers her father as the classic early-to-bed, early-to-rise type, sometimes getting up at 4 a.m. He usually went to bed around 8 p.m. "Your alarm clock," he would tell the girls, "that's opportunity knocking." His wee-morning hours would occasionally result in him catching one or more of his children trying to sneak in the house after a night of parties.

"We'd be coming in and he'd be up. He wouldn't say anything, he'd just look at you," said SuSu Gordy, the eldest of the five children.

He often would go to work at his Fairvilla office — the headquarters for the soda pop empire — little more than a mile from home on Sunday mornings while the family went to church.

Gator spent a summer at the Puerto Rico plant, too, doing manual work, such as stacking pallets and lugging fifty-pound sacks of sugar. Tom had a similar experience in 1976.

The new plant, where the cans were folded, was called the Carolina Canning Company and it sold to the filling plant next door called Caribbean Food Products.

Brown Sr., never stopped tinkering and going over his product lines and profit margins. Eventually, he decided that the real money was not in the soda pop, but the canning. So, he sold all his soda pop plants and went all in with canning at the plant in Puerto Rico, where he was given investment incentives by the government.

An *Orlando Sentinel* article said he sold four plants to Shasta in a "multi-million dollar transaction." Shasta, in a company newsletter, said the "plants have high-speed canning lines...and also pack 28 oz. bottles."

Brown Sr., in a March, 1968 interview with the trade publication *The American Soft Drink Journal*, said he also sold a plant to Coca-Cola, the price not revealed. FFP, he said, was trying to become more efficient and was computerizing existing operations.

Gator and Holson remember the high-tech push. FFP, they said, was among the first companies in Central Florida to begin the switch from pencil-and-paper payroll accounting ledgers to computers. Brown Sr., teamed up with the Duda farming conglomerate in Oviedo to make the change, transmitting data over phone lines. The transition was not easy, with payroll records fouled up in the beginning, Gator said.

## BEVERAGE BUSINESS STARTS TO SHIFT

During the early 1970s, Brown Sr., purchased new canning equipment for the Puerto Rico operation. Unfortunately for Brown Sr., a problem developed with the sealing function. The result was that beverages he had canned for clients all over the region began sprouting leaks within a few months of delivery, ruining all of the inventory.

His business was devastated. He and the canning machinery manufacturer sued each other, each blaming the other for the debacle. The suits lingered in the courts for years with no real resolution. Hyperinflation, meanwhile, was taking hold throughout the decade, dragging down the economy by driving up consumer prices as well as interest rates. Peaking at more than 13 percent in 1980, inflation drove up the cost of borrowing money so much that many businesses, including FFP, virtually ground to a halt.

FFP was doing so poorly that Brown Sr., thought about filing bankruptcy, but did not, Gator said. As a precaution, he deeded two small plots of citrus he owned to a longtime friend, Chester Karst, who ran one of the largest grove-care businesses in the state. Karst eventually gave him the deeds back.

Money in the Brown household became tight, so much so that when SuSu was marrying Bruce Gordy in 1975, there was no liquor at the reception. Everyone assumed it was because Brown Sr., was accommodating Gordy's father, a Baptist minister. It wasn't until years later that Caroline Brown told her daughter that the real reason was they were trying to economize.

"We never knew when we had a little (money) or a lot. It was all the same," said SuSu, a homemaker.

Later that year, Brown Sr., had a heart attack while undergoing bypass surgery at Vanderbilt University. He was fifty three. It was the beginning of a slow downward spiral that would last twenty years.

"He was my hero, as was my mother. Who can say that about both their parents?" Holson said.

Brown Sr., his daughters said, would not argue about minute details, preferring to focus on the big picture. Were the kids responsible? Was the business making money? "I'm not going to live my life with nitpicking," Brenda recalled him saying. "He didn't like the little stuff."

Tom, at the time, was at Bishop Moore High School, just a few miles from the Orlando Country Club. Gator, who had attended a year of college at Texas Christian University, had transferred to the University of Florida and was soon to drop out because he had tired of school. He told his mother and father about his plans one evening as they were enjoying an evening cocktail on their back porch overlooking the golf course.

"Dad, I'm kinda burned out," said Gator, explaining his decision to abandon college.

Brown Sr., replied: "You can stay here for three weeks. Then you're on your own."

Gator found a masonry job at the then-Orlando Naval Training Center and rented a small house with a friend. That lasted about a year.

"Dad was good about it," Gator said. "Everybody has their own timeline for their journey."

Gator eventually tired of manual labor in the scorching summer heat of Central Florida and returned to school, earning a degree in food and resource economics. His graduation present was a round-trip ticket to England, a journey that was supposed to last two weeks, but turned into a two-year sojourn around the world.

# 7

## THE GAME CHANGER – ALOE

### BROTHERS TAKE CHANCE ON CITRUS ALTERNATIVE

Overseas adventures behind them, Gator and Tom Brown slowly settled in at Florida Food Products, showing up each workday morning, trying to figure out ways to get the company on the move again.

The year was 1983 and Gator had been on the job for three years, while Tom had just joined the team during the early fall, following his overseas adventures. Their brother Bill, who goes by the nickname Hoe, was on the payroll, too, taking care of the groves. He would eventually leave FFP to follow his interest in real estate development in Tampa.

Tom was filling in on jobs around the company, getting reacquainted with the operations. Usually, he was in the groves tending to the trees or in the plant. Gator typically was in the office, wracking his brain to expand FFP's business line beyond grove maintenance, warehouse storage and the rapidly declining citrus processing segment of the portfolio.

Gator had spent the previous two years working with his

dad to launch Orange Scream, a drink concocted by Lakeland juice marketer Julian Fussell that blended citrus and milk. Fussell had trademarked the name in May 1980. The plan was to break into the school market with a sweet, nutritious drink that kids would clamor for rather than a Coke or Mountain Dew. Gator also tried to sell Orange Scream to soft-serve ice cream companies.

The drink tasted similar to an orange cremesicle and was inexpensive to produce because FFP would be able to tap into the federal government's vast reserves of cheap powdered milk as one of the primary ingredients. It was an early attempt by the Browns to take a product largely ignored or undervalued — powdered milk, in this case — and transform it into a moneymaker.

But despite their best efforts, Orange Scream went nowhere, forcing Brown Sr., to end the trial as the losses escalated, even though Gator wanted to keep trying. Brown Sr., though, had seen enough. It was time to move on, though to what no one was quite sure.

"We were pretty down. We were broke."

— JERRY "GATOR" BROWN

One spring morning shortly after Orange Scream's demise, the phone rang at Gator's desk, interrupting his new product ruminations. He picked up the receiver to hear the voice of a manager at the now-defunct Golden Gem citrus cooperative about two miles south from FFP in Orange County.

"Can you guys process aloe vera?" she asked.

"Sure," replied Gator, who wasn't quite sure what aloe vera was, much less if FFP had the capability of processing it.

"Great," she said. "We can't do it, but I have the name and number of a company looking for some help. Give them a call."

The inquiry to Golden Gem had come from Terry Laboratories in Melbourne, Florida. The company was trying to get into — or essentially launch — an aloe vera line. It was seeking an operation that could process the raw aloe plant into concentrate or powder that could be reconstituted into a drink or lotion. Terry Labs would sell to wholesalers, who would customize the product and court the retail side of the business.

Gator quickly said yes, then started researching aloe vera to figure out what he had gotten FFP into. That task wasn't so easy during the early 1980s, when the internet was still in development and far from the one touch of a key on a laptop computer or iPad that it is now. Gator had to make calls to experts and find printed literature.

What he learned was that the name aloe vera was derived for the Arabic word halal, which means "bitter and shiny substance." A perennial succulent grown in warm climates, such as Southern Arabia, Central America and the Caribbean, aloe has stiff, fleshy leaves that contain a translucent inner pulp and the resinous yellow aloin.

It was used for centuries for its medicinal properties, going all the way back to ancient China, as well as ancient Egypt.

Both those societies used the lotion to soothe wounds and burns, as well as to reduce fever. Among the earliest proponents were Alexander the Great and Cleopatra. Closer to home, Floridians had grown it in their gardens for decades, if not all the way back to the 1700s, using it for homeopathic remedies such as a topical ointment for sunburn.

Studies Gator found indicated aloe rubbed on the skin could inhibit infection and aid in the healing of minor burns, wounds and frostbite. It could help with psoriasis and seborrheic dermatitis, too.

Drinking aloe also can improve what's commonly referred to now as gut health, according to some researchers. Liquid aloe, proponents contend, can alleviate indigestion, stomach ulcers, colitis, hemorrhoids, urinary tract infections and other related maladies.

All that sounded good to Gator, who thought there could be a demand for such a product in what was then a nascent healthy-living market. He looked over the specs of the plant's equipment and determined the machinery could, indeed, process aloe after some adjustments were made.

The first step for FFP was scraping up the cash to recalibrate its equipment to handle aloe, not citrus. They were busy making the transition when the Christmas Eve freeze of 1983 hit.

Frigid air from Canada blew into the state that night, dropping temperatures from the mid-fifties down to the twenties within three hours, shortly after the sun went down. Temperatures kept falling through the night and early morning, dipping into the teens in some regions. By daybreak Christmas Day, much of the citrus industry was devastated. A high percentage of the crop — especially in Central Florida — was frozen, meaning it had to be processed in a hurry before it spoiled.

## FREEZE PAYS FOR ALOE VERA CONVERSION

FFP switched gears at the plant and took in all the oranges it could, turning them into concentrate as fast as the company's old evaporator and pulp dryers would work. The freeze made FFP's financial year, pulling the company out of its funk and placing plenty of money back in the reserve account. But Gator, Tom and Brown Sr., knew counting on freezes was not a sustainable business model.

The company spent three months strictly processing oranges before going back to aloe vera, using some of the freeze profits to finance the switch. After processing two loads of aloe leaves from Texas for Terry Laboratories, the Browns had seen enough to believe the product could be a money-maker. They decided to get into the market themselves and hired Tim Meadows, a cosmetics chemist from Terry Labs, to help with the transition and sales.

At first, FFP toyed with the idea of trying to grow aloe on old citrus groves it owned south of Winter Garden, but the Browns quickly learned labor costs were too high and the weather too iffy. They located an aloe grower in Texas, allowing FFP to start experimenting with the product. They shipped the raw leaves to Eustis — not an easy task since it takes 400 pounds of leaves to make just one pound of powder. Aloe, in its natural form, is 99.5 percent water.

A freeze hit Texas during the mid-1980s, forcing FFP to

look to another source for aloe. Brown Sr., knew some people in the Dominican Republic, so FFP set up shop there, investing about $600,000 made during the freeze in two mobile trailers that would use reverse osmosis to concentrate the aloe, greatly reducing shipping costs because they were not moving the leaves anymore. One trailer would extract the aloe, while the other would partially concentrate it enough to ship back to Eustis for the final processing.

Tom became the company aloe salesman about that time, but it was a slow start. Most people were like Gator. They did not know what aloe was, much less what it was good for. One of Tom's biggest jobs was education. Along with Meadows, Tom had to tell potential customers the aloe vera story before he could sell it. They knocked on countless doors, trying to quickly get to the health benefits before the potential buyer lost interest.

The first break came when Schering-Plough agreed to buy aloe. A New Jersey-based pharmaceutical company, Schering-Plough was known for manufacturing allergy drugs like Claritin and Clarinex, but it also was diversified, owning the Dr. Scholl's foot care brand, as well as the Coppertone skincare line. Coppertone was the sweet spot for the Browns. Schering-Plough decided to put aloe vera into its sunblock products, as well as aftercare items treating sunburn, such as Solarcaine.

Fruit of the Earth, which was selling skincare products to the rapidly growing Walmart chain, came on board. That made aloe vera the first big hit for the young Brown brothers. Other contracts followed, including ones from L'Oréal, Johnson & Johnson, Merck and Royal Canin.

Seeking to cut expenses and improve the aloe quality, the

Browns moved the operation for a year or two to Costa Rica. But labor costs again proved too high, plus they had to battle flooding from heavy rains.

## GUASTATOYA BECOMES ALOE BASE

Guatemala became the next and , what would prove to be, the final stop for aloe and FFP. Brown Sr., scouted out the location after talking to a man named Alfredo Olivia. "I think we've got someone we can work with," Brown Sr., told his sons.

The Browns built a 5,000-square-foot plant during 1990 in a rural town called Guastatoya, the capital of the department state of El Progreso. Located about fifty miles east from the city of Guatemala, Guastatoya is home to the Guastatoya Water Park, a popular area attraction. FFP soon became the town's largest employer, with eighty to ninety full-time plant workers, not including the twenty-five or so small farmers who grew the plants and laborers who harvested the leaves.

By the time FFP arrived in Guatemala, the company had strong sales and a good reputation in the market. By 1996, the company was processing 6,000 tons of aloe annually at the Guatemala plant, filleting the eighteen-inch leaves by hand. The key to success for FFP was offering a clean product, one that wasn't adulterated or cut with cheap fillers like powdered corn starch, or maltodextrin, and other juice solids that pad the bottom line but dilute the quality.

"That's (adulteration) very profitable to scumbags," said Oliver Anderson, who worked eleven years with FFP, from 2001-2012. His job was selling aloe all over the world, often traveling with Tom Brown. As much as 80 percent of the sales were overseas, with particularly strong demand in Europe and Korea.

Anderson joked that some products made by competitors contained so little aloe that consumers would be just as well off rubbing the plastic container on their skin as the contents. "They both had the same amount of aloe. None," Anderson said.

A 2016 investigation of the aloe market by *Bloomberg News* found store-brand aloe products at Target, CVS and Walmart contained no aloe at all. According to *Bloomberg,* studies of the products determined the chemical maltodextrin rather than aloe was in the products. Maltodextrin is a cheap chemical agent that imitates the qualities of aloe.

A report by the independent research company ConsumerLab in 2015 discovered similar results by finding that only half of the aloe products it tested had the expected levels of aloe.

FFP got out of the aloe business in 2013 largely because the demand for another product line — celery powder — had exploded. Not only was celery powder much more profitable than aloe, it also was consuming the majority of the Brown brothers' time. They sold their aloe vera customer list to Pharmtec and the Guatemala plant to Concentrated Aloe Corp.

The quality of FFP's aloe was never questioned or came up short, Anderson said, largely because Gator and Tom were deeply involved in the day-to-day operations and would not cheat. "They (competitors) couldn't duplicate FFP quality," he said.

Early in the development phase of aloe, Gator said, he talked to his dad about throwing in some additives as a way to improve company finances. Brown Sr., was adamant in saying no. "Once you go down that road," he told Gator, "you can't go back. We've got to stick with it."

True to the words of Brown Sr., Tom and Gator made sure the aloe stayed pure, Anderson said. "They were always watching," he said. "They were hands on. They were always there."

Keith Burt, who worked for FFP for thirty years, hired on in 1988 as an aloe technician. For many years, Burt was one of the key employees working on aloe, ensuring it met quality standards and troubleshooting at the Guastatoya plant.

He would fly to Guatemala four to six times a year to make sure the plant was operating properly and to tinker with, or tweak, machinery to improve performance. The Browns, he said, never stopped experimenting.

"They were always looking for something else, different processes, ways for making the equipment work. That's my style, too, learning new things, trying new things," said Burt, who met his wife Telma Castañón in Guastatoya. Castañón was FFP's comptroller in Guatemala.

The plant was situated in the middle of fields of aloe farmed by various owners. FFP owned 150 acres of aloe, which provided about 40 percent of the plant's needs. The rest came from local aloe farmers, many of them growing the plants on tracts of five acres or less. The Browns typically financed the upfront costs for the smaller operations. The plant ran around the clock six days a week during the processing season, closing only during the dry months of May through July.

## TROUBLE CROPS UP IN GUASTATOYA

In 2005, Gator and Tom were going over the books and noticed the employee count was rising at the operation, but it was not accompanied by an increase in production. "I said, 'Something doesn't feel right,'" Gator recalled.

He started looking at the payroll records with Burt and they figured out that the plant manager and the manager of the local bank that held the FFP account had come up with a scam. The plant manager was relatively new, having replaced the original manager, Oscar Bernardini, who had died of a brain aneurysm. Bernardini's replacement and the banker had teamed up to add phantom employees to the payroll, then split the proceeds of the checks between them after cashing them, Gator and Burt surmised. After consulting with Tom and Burt, Gator decided what needed to be done, but he knew it was not going to be easy.

He flew down to Guastatoya, booked a room at the local hotel, then hustled up a couple of armed bodyguards in case his plan met with more resistance than he anticipated. "I didn't know what was going to happen," Gator said.

Guards in tow, Gator went to the plant and called for a meeting of all employees — usually between eighty and ninety people — between the first and second shifts. He fired the plant manager, whose first name was Ivan. "He started crying. He was upset," Gator said. "He was crooked as hell." Gator then told everyone that he was shutting down the operation immediately and not re-opening it until he could get the books and payroll back in order.

Three months passed as Gator, Tom and Burt devised a much more professional way of dealing with workers and payroll. They came up with an employee handbook that spelled out wages and benefits, pledged to protect the environment and committed that 10 percent of the sales to participating customers would be re-invested in the community.

Over time, FFP spent more than $250,000 on a variety of projects in and around Guastatoya. Among them were: purchasing school supplies for students, drilling numerous community wells, underwriting sustainable family gardens, investing in poultry farming, repairing and installing windows in a school, contributing to a water purification system and buying stoves to replace wood-burning fire pits for family meals. In all, 862 families were affected by the program, FFP records indicated.

The Browns figured if the workers understood that the company was committed to Guastatoya, they would be more likely to stop any future frauds. Quite simply, they had to understand that cheating FFP was the same as cheating themselves.

The employees liked the new program, which the Browns dubbed "Community Trade." Its principles, particularly the local reinvestment of profits, was adopted by other companies, including in the marketing campaign of the Body Shop, one of FFP's major aloe clients. Illustrations of Guastatoya farmers were posted in Body Shop retail shops throughout Europe and the United States.

Telma Castañón, who was the plant accountant in Guastatoya, said the FFP plant brought prosperity to a region that had "a horrible level of under-nutrition, unemployment and extreme poorness." The aloe-processing plant, she said, created "a day and night experience for many families during the years. We know for sure the benefit of a permanent and a decent income was for at least seventy-five families, and I would say for the total community with the indirect invest."

Gator and Tom, she said, were well respected in Guastatoya. Residents, she said, "trust in the company and in the owners, the Brown brothers, each time, we mention 'Mr. Brown needs...' everybody committed with all that we request."

When the Browns said they were selling, Castañón said, "the shock and sadness (of the employees) was so intense from the absolute silence to the tears."

But outside forces had begun to play on Guastatoya that were beyond the control of the Browns. The place became increasingly dangerous because it was turning into a crossroads for the drug trade and coyotes, or criminals who smuggle undocumented immigrants from Central America into the United States.

Cocaine and marijuana were passing through the community in increasing quantities, creating an old Wild West atmosphere in Guastatoya. Guns abounded. There were killings linked to the drugs and human trafficking. The local media even published stories about newborns being bought and sold in the area.

Gator and Tom decided the best course of action was to dress down, not flash money or wear jewelry when in town. They wanted to avoid drawing attention. Bottom line: They tended to the plant and kept to themselves. "As long as you didn't mess with them," Gator said, "they didn't mess with you."

## REGRET: ALOE VERA WAS NOT A HULA HOOP

Though aloe vera very likely saved FFP from going out of business, the Brown brothers were always of the belief that the product was nothing more than a fad. "We never really went all in. We thought it was a hula hoop," Tom said of the leafy plant they processed and sold for more than twentyfive years.

In retrospect, both say they should have invested more heavily in aloe and marketing it to customers. Aloe, after all, has remained a staple in a variety of skin and health care products. Globally, aloe sales were estimated at $13 billion in 2012 and expected to grow, according to the International Aloe Science Council.

But celery powder eventually became the No. 1 product of FFP, overwhelming everything else because of the rising demand and accompanying profits. "We were pulling our hair out," Gator said of the ever-increasing workload. But, Gator added about the aloe plant, "It was like green gold to us."

❧

## 8

## CARROT REDUX

### LEVERAGING THE CULLS

Tom would fly to Korea or Japan every three months or so working on aloe sales, meeting with the same people over and over to build his relationships with them. The get-togethers, he concluded, seemed to be as much about trust and talking one on one as they were about the product or making a sales pitch. That, Tom had learned during the mid-1980s, was the Asian way of doing business.

During one flight back home, he was seated next to an older American. They started conversing to pass the time during the 15.5-hour flight from Seoul, South Korea to Orlando International Airport.

The discussion turned to work and Tom, sitting next to the window, explained he was part of a family business that owned a food-ingredients processing plant in Eustis. They were struggling, Tom said, to leave citrus behind and diversify into other lines with the growth potential oranges lacked. The company had moved into aloe vera, he said, but that wasn't enough to offset the loss of citrus, which, Tom said bluntly, was dying.

"I've got the answer to your problem. Call me when you get back to the office," said the man, who handed Tom a card and introduced himself as Ferd LeGrand, an agronomist at the University of Florida.

Tom followed up with a phone call a few days later and, in a scene reminiscent of the classic 1960s movie *The Graduate*, LeGrand offered Tom one word about the product of the future for Florida Food Products. But instead of uttering "plastics" LeGrand simply said, "carrots."

LeGrand, at the time, was a consultant with Long Farms near Lake Apopka. They were one of several farms growing vegetables in the organically rich and fertile muck fields along the north shore of Lake Apopka, just a few miles south of the FFP plant in Eustis.

Like their fellow growers, Long was struggling about what to do with the carrots they grew that did not meet strict cosmetic standards for sale as fresh produce. Depending on the weather and other conditions, 20 to 50 percent of their carrot crop could be ruled substandard, rendering them unsalable.

Though there actually was nothing intrinsically wrong with the carrots, their fatal flaw was they were not visually perfect. Instead of being straight, with a full tail and tapered shaft, they might be crooked, blemished or discolored. That made them culls in the estimation of grocery stores and consumers. Instead of throwing them away or plowing them under, the usual practice for the growers was to virtually donate the culls to ranchers for cattle feed.

LeGrand suggested that FFP turn the culls into juice, concentrate or powder. Carrots, he said, are loaded with beta carotenes and are a precursor to Vitamin A, which possesses antioxidant characteristics that fight cancer and the effects of aging. Asians, research showed, were big into antioxidants. So why not sell them — and the good, old U.S.A., for that matter — carrots in juice, concentrate or powder form?

His advice made sense to Tom, who conducted some research and learned that beta carotenes are good for eyesight and helping maintain the membranes in your nose and respiratory tract. Breaking it down further, he found that one small, raw carrot contains 8,353 international units of Vitamin A. That meant eating one carrot provided more than 200 times the recommended daily intake of Vitamin A. Even better, one cup of carrot juice contained more beta carotene than a cup of any other food. What's not to like, right? Tom reasoned.

## TURNING CULLS FROM CATTLE FEED TO MONEY

Tom sold his brother and Brown Sr., on the carrot idea and they approached the Lake Apopka muck growers, dropping LeGrand's name to get in the door and then offering to take the culls off their collective hands. The basic pitch: Something (cash) for nothing (carrots). It proved persuasive. Eventually, they made a deal with Zellwin Farms, Clonts Farms, Hooper Farms, Long Farms and Lust Farms.

Charlie Kennedy, the vice president of Zellwin Farms Co., said his company was happy to work with the Browns. "We were always open to new ideas," he said.

At the time, Zellwin was growing carrots on 2,000 acres, producing the annual equivalent of 75,000 fifty-pound bags of carrots. That meant Zellwin had to practically give away thousands of pounds of carrots each year because the look was less than ideal.

The Brown agreement stipulated that FFP would conduct product development, transport and process the carrots and, most importantly, sell them to beverage and cosmetic companies. The farms would share in the profits, minus the processing fee and related expenses. As they did with aloe vera, the Browns and their FFP employees wasted little time before tweaking the machinery and getting to work.

"We did a few truckloads, started screwing around with it. Learned the tricks," Gator said.

The key for the Brown brothers was they figured out a way to "cloud stabilize" the carrot juice, or make sure nothing fell to the bottom of the drink, which was especially noticeable in glass containers. "That's what really set us apart," Tom said. "Consumers didn't want anything on the bottom."

The proprietary technology they developed included suspending the insoluble beta carotene (lipid) in the liquid, yielding an illuminated bright carrot color in the beverage. The process deactivated plant enzymes in the raw carrot and then again in the juice, rendering the drink perfectly cloud stable, Tom said. Nothing on the bottom, in other words.

FFP then purchased more drying equipment to allow the company to move into more powdered offerings, such as dehydrated citrus juice powders for sale in markets similar to its aloe line of products. Soon, FFP was selling orange, pineapple, grape, lemon, lime, strawberry, raspberry and mandarin concentrated powders, promoting them as whole food dietary supplements.

Later, FFP sold to a direct-television marketing firm called HumanN, which promotes a beet crystal product called Beet-Elite as an athletic-performance enhancer. BeetElite is sold to customers directly and is advertised nationally under the brand name SuperBeets. The sales pitch is based on studies that indicate the natural nitrates in beets, when converted to nitrites ($NO_2$), can help people run, bike and exercise longer. The theory is the beet juice or powder — once mixed with water and consumed — expands blood vessels, allowing the user to burn less energy while exercising due to the elevated metabolization of oxygen, thus increasing stamina. Cut through the jargon and athletes saw one thing: Drinking the stuff might give me an advantage.

Tom sold the carrot juice to similar customers he had developed for aloe, figuring both products were for the health conscious. His instincts proved correct. FFP customers succeeded in their retail sales by promoting the high plant nutrient content contained in daily servings of carrot and other vegetable juices. One of the first and biggest buyers from FFP was Kagome, Japan's largest tomato processing company.

Before long, Korea and Japan became huge markets for all types of juices, especially carrot, in part because Tom already had made numerous connections through his aloe sales. "They got going pretty good, pretty strong. We worked those markets pretty hard," Gator said.

The learning curve for aloe and carrots led FFP to start

juicing, concentrating or turning into a powder all manner of vegetables, including cabbage, celery, cucumbers, kale, green bell peppers, mushrooms, onions, parsley and spinach.

The additional sales income allowed FFP to hire lab researchers to develop even more products, including a concentrated blend of clarified carrot, celery and onion that combined to make a highly flavored, natural mirepoix base, or vegetable stock. It was used to replace MSG, or monosodium glutamate, a flavor enhancer commonly used in Chinese food during the 1980s. MSG fell into disfavor because of the notion that large doses of it could cause headaches in people eating food with the supplement. Healthy Choice, owned by the food conglomerate Conagra, bought the FFP mirepoix for use in numerous soups and prepared foods.

Citrus and vegetable juice powder sales grew and FFP added millions of dollars of drying capacity to meet demand. The dryers, forty feet long and eight feet in diameter, removed the water using vacuum. A state-of-the-art, humidity-controlled room for dry-packing operations also was installed.

The beet powder, Veg Dry Carrot, FFP produced became a hit as well. It first was shipped to the AIM Companies, a multi-level marketing operation based in Nampa, Idaho. AIM is similar to the Amway Co. in its sales and marketing. But instead of peddling health, beauty, and home care products, AIM Companies specialized in nutritional items. AIM products Just Carrots and Just Beets were based on FFP supplies of Veg Dry Carrot and Veg Dry Beet.

Carrot juice and aloe vera, though, were among the biggest winners for the Browns, enough to propel the company far from the brink of ruin during the early 1980s. By 1996, the company annually was processing 10,000 tons of carrots and 6,000 tons of aloe leaf equivalent at the Eustis plant.

## CARROT PLANT BUILT IN WASHINGTON STATE

But there was a problem with carrots. And it wasn't their looks. The state of Florida had announced its intention during the mid-1990s to buy the muck farms along the north shore of Lake Apopka. The reason: pesticide and fertilizer runoff from the farms had virtually destroyed Florida's fourth-largest lake. Once renowned for its abundance of bass fish, the almost 31,000-acre lake was choking on algae blooms, stripping the water of the oxygen and sunlight needed to keep plants and fish alive.

Environmentalists argued the only way to restore the lake was to stop the runoff by going after the source – the very farms that were supplying carrots to the Browns.

So, in 1995, FFP opened a multi-million dollar plant in rural Washington state to process carrots there in an effort to keep up with demand for their product, as well as to create a secondary supply if the muck farms were taken away by the state. The Browns struck a  deal with two different Washington farms for culls. But carrots from one farm — about two miles from the plant — were not delivered reliably, with production spotty and the quality poor.

"Those things were like mush," Charlie Hamrick said of the carrots. Hamrick, who helped set up the Washington plant, worked more than forty years with the Browns before retiring in 2011.

The carrots essentially were blanched — not fresh — upon arrival, making processing difficult, Hamrick said. But Hamrick — described by Tom as a practical thinker and innovative tinkerer — devised some workarounds to keep the plant going.

## TRAGEDY STRIKES

Though Gator and Tom were making virtually all the deals and running the operation by the mid 1990s, they still consulted almost daily with their father. He would come in to work most days for a few hours, maybe go to lunch with them or friends.

But Brown Sr., was not the robust man who had fought in World War II and founded and run Florida Food Products for decades on his own. His health had been slipping for years, going back to a heart attack he suffered in 1972 while undergoing bypass surgery at Vanderbilt University. He had a second attack three years later at home.

From the time Gator and Tom had hired on, Brown Sr., had taught them what he knew, slowing ceding authority to them.

"He would let us make mistakes, but not big ones."

— TOM BROWN

Brown Sr. was glad to have his sons take over. "His day had come and was passing by," said Don Bailey, who worked in management from 1992-97 with FFP. Tom and Gator respected Bailey for his work ethic and considered him akin to a brother.

Gator was much like his father, Bailey said, knowing all

about what was going on in the plant. But over time, Bailey said, Gator might even have surpassed his father in his management abilities. "He liked to keep his hands on everything, a lot like his father," Bailey said.

Brown Sr., and his eldest son, Bailey said, were much the same in that, "You never had to guess where they were on something. They would tell you, 'Keep going or stop doing it.'"

The pair had strong opinions as well. "I heard a lot of shouting matches," Bailey said. "You had two strong-willed individuals. You'd hear 'Dad we can't do it that way anymore.'"

Tom, meanwhile, was either in the Washington plant or traveling throughout Asia and Europe, selling to food manufacturers, along with supporting FFP's international and domestic distributors. He stayed in contact with the Eustis plant by Western Union telex during the early days. Tom, too, exhibited plenty of his father's traits, including perseverance. Bailey described Tom as a "hard, tireless" worker. "Once he has an idea, he has a laser focus on it," Bailey said. "He'll ride that horse as long as it will go."

Despite differences of opinions on company strategy or tactics, there never was any question about the affection Gator, Tom and Brown Sr. shared. "They loved each other fiercely and fought fiercely," Bailey said.

Brown Sr., however, had a weak heart, just like his father, Alexander Z Brown. A fertilizer salesman who lived in Winter Garden, Alexander Z Brown died in 1934 of a heart attack while driving his car to the hospital because he was feeling ill. He was fifty-four years old. Unlike his father's abrupt end, Brown Sr., faded slowly.

By the spring of 1995, he was too weak to do much more than get out of bed. He agreed to have Hospice come to the house for his final days because he did not want to burden Caroline, his wife of forty-six years, said their oldest daughter, SuSu Gordy.

"Is that going to make it easier for your mother?" he asked SuSu and her sister, Brenda Holson. He was lying in bed and they were seated next to him. Both nodded yes. "That's a great idea," he told them. Hospice was brought in within hours.

SusSu Gordy said the family would sit with Brown Sr. in shifts, ensuring he would not be alone. She was with him Sunday, May 14, 1995. It was Mother's Day. He was drifting in and out of consciousness, saying little, yet cognizant of his surroundings, SuSu recalled. But she noticed his breathing was becoming shallower and more sporadic. She could feel him slipping away, so she called in her mother. SuSu left, allowing her mother to be alone with her husband.

Jerry Brown Sr., died quietly in his Orlando home, 1209 Country Lane, hard by the tenth green, Caroline at his side. In healthier, earlier times, he likely would have been at work at his old office a mile away, poring over the books or plotting another deal.

"He was my hero, as was my mother. Who can say that about both their parents?" Brenda said.

Brown Sr., was remembered in newspaper accounts as a leader in citrus, banking and food processing. One of his associates in the citrus industry, Jim Bock, was quoted in the *Winter Garden Times* saying, "Jerry Brown was a fellow who had an inquisitive mind and was always thinking ahead."

He was buried at Woodlawn Memorial Park, Orlando.

Gator and Tom, like their mother and siblings, were devastated. Not only had they lost their father, but their work mentor and chief business adviser was gone, too. They felt lost. "What would Dad do?" was the thought that often crossed the minds of Tom and Gator.

"It was hard," Tom said, "really hard."

## TIME RUNS OUT ON MUCK FARMS

Regardless of personal sorrow, the business world did not wait for Tom and Gator to recover. They had plenty of pressing issues facing them, most prominently that the state of Florida was about to put the muck farmers out of business.

The Florida Legislature concluded in 1996 that it was time to start the cleanup of Lake Apopka. So it started negotiating with the farmers to buy the land. Eventually, the state spent $200 million buying almost 20,000 acres of muck farms during the late 1990s and started the long process of restoring the land to its natural wetland state. The five farms that the Browns had contracted with were no longer growing carrots.

"Once they (the state) got into it, you didn't have a choice," said Kennedy, whose farm closed in 1998. Zellwin now manufactures egg cartons and boxes.

The biggest fear for the Browns was that they could not fulfill their supply obligations, possibly setting them up for costly breach-of-contract lawsuits. Gator and Tom huddled, talked over the possibilities. The one certainty they faced was they needed more carrots — tons of them, in fact — and they had to have them now.

"It was really beyond the scope of FFP's ability to supply," Bailey said.

"It (the carrot market) really took off. We weren't ready for it," Tom said. "We knew we had problems."

Bailey, who specialized in carrots and vegetables for FFP, said, "It went crazy. It grew so fast."

Once again, the Browns did some research. Gator learned that just about the largest carrot grower in the country was the then-family-owned Bolthouse Farms in Bakersfield, California. That was all he needed to know.

He caught the next flight out of Orlando International and headed to California's Central Valley. Not wasting any time, he went straight to the company headquarters and asked to see the owner, William Bolthouse, who was part of the fourth generation of the family to run the operation. Not surprisingly, Gator was told to wait in the lobby. "They didn't know us from squat," Gator said.

A marketing manager, Tom McCorkle, came out to meet Gator, asked what the visit was about and whether he could help. Gator politely told him that he only wanted to meet with Mr. Bolthouse and would wait for however long it might take for him to be free a few moments to talk. After two hours, Gator was informed by the receptionist to come back tomorrow, though there were no guarantees he could see Bolthouse then. Since he had no other option, Gator got a hotel room nearby and returned the next day. Bolthouse finally brought Gator into his office, triggering three days of negotiations.

## GATOR MAKES A DEAL WITH BOLTHOUSE FARMS

"We hit it off. It was lucky. We jived," Gator said of Bolthouse.

Bailey, now the director of global sales for Bolthouse Farms, was not surprised that Gator and the elder Bolthouse would enjoy each other's company. Both, he said, speak directly and to the point and are men of their word.

"They would say, 'Let's cut through the bull and get to what we want to talk about,'" Bailey said. Gator, he added, was a good negotiator, a trait he learned from his father. "He (Gator) had a way of getting information from people that you wouldn't normally get," Bailey said.

Gator's intent from the start was to sell FFP's entire carrot operation, including the Washington state plant, to Bolthouse. But he needed some negotiating room, so he started off by trying to enter into a partnership with Bolthouse.

First, he laid out all the benefits of the carrot juice market, how it was exploding in popularity, especially the unexpectedly strong rollout of Campbell Soup's V8 Splash, which was based on carrot juice. FFP had secured a three-year assignable contract for V8 Splash, which had maxed out the Brown's ability to produce carrot juice.

So, Gator summarized, let us build a plant on Bolthouse property in the Valley and we'll take all of your useless culls and pretty much process them into money.

"I always thought those (cull) carrots were for the bung hole," Bolthouse replied.

Gator was confident he had made a good pitch. Bolthouse, after all, was following the Lake Apopka model by almost giving away its culled carrots for cattle feed, selling them for ten dollars to twenty dollars per ton to ranchers in the San Joaquin Valley. Bolthouse, which had 200 to 500 tons of waste daily, was only selling whole carrots and just starting to capitalize on the rapidly growing and more lucrative cut-and-peeled and ready-to-eat variety. The concept of juicing was foreign to them.

"Jerry, that's interesting," Bolthouse said to Gator at the end of his proposal.

Bolthouse paused for a moment, Gator said, before pulling the drapes away from a large picture window in his office. It overlooked a massive warehouse and plant, one Gator estimated covered 400,000 square feet. Surrounding the plants was carrot fields as far as the eye could see. There were 15,000 acres of carrots, in fact.

"Where do you think we would put it?" Bolthouse asked.

That, Gator said, "was his (Bolthouse's) way of saying, 'We're taking you out or it's nothing.'"

The two went back and forth for three days, with Tom involved by phone. They came to a basic agreement, though the actual contract would have to be hammered out later by attorneys for both sides. "It was kind of a principle thing, on a notepad," Gator said.

Eventually, Gator would return one more time with Tom to close the deal together.

The pending pact was reminiscent of the way Brown Sr., would make deals. Often, Gator said, his dad would write something down on the back of a cocktail napkin or slip of paper. Those scribblings, he said, would form the foundation of a deal, just like Gator did with Bolthouse.

In essence, Gator described the deal as, "We'll teach you

about juicing. You'll get the customers and the plant." In return, Gator said, the Browns were paid a lump sum, plus 5 percent royalties off the first three years of sale. The royalties were critical in the later development of a natural watermelon-based insect attractant, which became a big seller for the company.

Included in the pact was the promise to move the Washington state plant to Bakersfield. That took six months and was spearheaded by Hamrick.

Bailey was in charge of teaching Bolthouse the juicing business. Part of Bailey's duties was writing all the operation specifications, including on such minute details as pH levels, acidity and color. A Florida State graduate, Bailey has a degree in biological science and chemistry.

The Brown brothers speak highly of Bailey. "He brought a level of professionalism to us," Gator said. Added Tom: "Best salesman we ever had."

Bolthouse, in 2018, was expected to harvest and process 2,000 tons of carrots every day but Thanksgiving and Christmas. It is the largest producer of carrot juice, concentrate and fiber in the world.

The Bolthouse family sold out to a private equity firm, Madison Dearborn Partners, for an undisclosed price in 2005. That was shortly after Bolthouse launched its own line of branded juices. Madison Dearborn sold to Campbell Soup for $1.3 billion in 2012.

Bailey got to know the Bolthouses, whom he described as very religious, while helping them set up the carrot processing plant. He left the Browns and joined Bolthouse after the purchase became final.

In the end, Bailey said, the sale was completed because the Brown brothers were smart enough to take what many considered to be waste — culled carrots — and turn them into high quality, profitable products.

"Jerry and Tom were doing stuff that large companies just would not do."

— DON BAILEY, LONGTIME FFP MANAGER

## BROTHERS SOUGHT FOR BEETLE SOLUTION

Shortly before selling the carrot operation, the Browns were approached by Bob Bates, now a professor emeritus at the University of Florida. Bates had learned about cucurbitacin watermelons in Homestead and believed the bitter-tasting juice of the plant could be combined with a small amount of pesticide to kill an insect that was terrorizing corn farmers in the Midwest and Southwest. Bates was working with Robert Schroeder, an entomologist with the U.S. Department of Agriculture.

He called the Browns because they had a growing reputation as a creative company that was willing to take a chance. They had worked before with the school's Institute of Food and Agricultural Sciences and had previously welcomed the engineering school to come by as part of a plant production efficiencies study it was conducting.

Gator took the call from Bates and said yes, as he almost always did when he was offered an unusual proposition. "Ship us some watermelons," he told Bates, "and we'll figure out what to do with them."

The idea pitched by Bates and Schroeder was that corn rootworm beetles would be attracted to watermelon juice droplets applied to the corn plants. Throw a little pesticide in there — actually a lot less, as in 3.2 ounces per acre of methyl parathion versus the normal two pints per acre — and FFP just might have a highly coveted concoction to sell.

Made sense to Gator and Tom, so they went for it. At FFP, workers crushed the entire melon, turned it into concentrate formulated in soybean oil to help the mixture spread and stick on the corn leaf after it was sprayed from a low-flying plane.

Especially enticing to the Browns was the economics of the product they dubbed Invite. FFP spent fifteen dollars a gallon to make it, and would sell it for almost forty-three dollars a gallon.

Then it was up to Tom to sell to farmers in the Panhandle of Texas, western Kansas, eastern Colorado and much of Nebraska. He often drove a rented, red pickup truck because the University of Nebraska school colors are red and white. The bed of the truck typically was filled with five-gallon plastic pails of the watermelon-based pesticide.

Tom quickly figured out that he needed to win over crop consultants as opposed to knocking on the doors of countless farmers in the middle of nowhere. The consultants usually represented a collection of farmers and counseled them on the best ways to tend their crops, including the use of pesticides. Win over one consultant and you could pick up a dozen or more accounts.

To win his first few contracts, Tom basically gave away the

Invite. It was sprayed twice on the corn, once to kill the adults, the second time to destroy late-emerging beetles. That ensured that no laid eggs or resulting larvae were left to attack the corn roots the following year. Tom made his pitches to consultants in practically every diner from Fort Morgan, Colorado, to Garden City, Kansas, to Amarillo, Texas, to Omaha, Nebraska.

He ended up doing business with dozens of consultants, occasionally taking twenty or more of them from the modest, backroad diners to fishing trips in Costa Rica and even to a summer home the family owned on Lake Butler in west Orange County.

"I was walking the fields with them," he said of the consultants. "They were on my side, appreciating that an owner was walking fields counting beetles."

Eventually, word got around that Invite was the real deal, with sales going from 120 acres in south central Kansas in 2000 to more than 500,000 acres in 2001. Sales peaked at three million acres in the four-state region.

From 2000 to 2010, when FFP stopped selling Invite, Tom would fly out to the desert Southwest starting in July, a day or two after his July 4 birthday. He made the rounds, typically driving 6,000 miles before returning to his Winter Park home before Labor Day.

Invite came to an end because of three reasons: The federal EPA deemed methyl parathion too dangerous and took it off the market; researchers started genetically modifying corn to be resistant to the rootworm beetle; and farmers had to stop growing corn virtually year-round because they were pumping the underground Ogallala Aquifer dry to water the crop.

Farmers began rotating with crops such as soybeans and wheat, which required less water and prevented insects from multiplying.

"It was the most interesting and gratifying market experience of my career," Tom said.

More importantly, it bridged the gap to what would become the brothers' most lucrative venture.

# 9

# THE NATURAL CURE

## CELERY POWDER – A PARADIGM SHIFT

Gator and Tom Brown knew from their very first days at Florida Food Products that they had to get away from the struggling, contracting citrus industry if the company their dad had founded and built was going to survive, much less thrive, during the years ahead. Oranges, they concluded, represented the past. The brothers needed to find the future — and fast.

After joining the company in 1980 and 1983, respectively, the siblings continually experimented with and brought online a variety of foodstuffs that they would sell after turning them into juice, concentrate, powder or lotion. Products included aloe, carrots, beets, onions, bell peppers and even a watermelon extract they converted into a largely natural corn pesticide.

Most of their efforts were successful, but the pair came up with the occasional clunker, like the Orange Scream drink that combined orange juice with powdered milk. The Browns had hoped to sell the drink in schools as a nutritious alternative to soda pop, but could not break into the market.

Another failure was a plan during the early 2000s to compound natural color pigments for sale in the retail hair color business. The aim was to replace a suspected cancer-causing agent, para-pheylenediamine (PPD), found in artificial hair dyes.

The Browns set up a website to sell directly to consumers, a step they had never taken before. They quickly learned it was time consuming and complicated. They also discovered that the product they dubbed Vitacolor was not effective in 10 percent of the users, typically people whose hair was damaged from previous use of harsh dyes. The blogging world, which was then taking hold on the internet, caught onto the snafu and the reviews were harsh.

"We really didn't know what we were doing," Gator said. "It was a mistake."

The brothers decided to leave the business, absorbing a loss of about $750,000. The lesson they took away: "Bald brothers should not be selling hair color," Tom said.

Conversely, the biggest, most profitable ingredient they developed was celery powder.

FFP first began tinkering with celery during the late 1980s, turning it into a juice for use as a flavor enhancer. But it wasn't until the mid 2000s when they hit upon the highest, best and most lucrative use of celery.

It started with a phone call in 2005 from Jim Bacus, a bacteriologist from the University of Wisconsin who lives in Gainesville and is an adjunct professor at the University of

Florida. He was working for a Danish food company at the time, but was thinking of going out on his own because a discovery he had made about celery had been dismissed by his employer as something akin to a gimmick — a gimmick that eventually would help spawn a multi-billion dollar natural, processed-meat market segment.

Bacus had worked for decades with the meat industry and, starting during the late 1990s, noticed that organic and natural foods were becoming increasingly popular at places like the small, but expanding, Whole Foods supermarket chain.

The burgeoning organic/natural trend, he realized, was a problem for the makers of processed meats such as bacon, pepperoni, hot dogs and deli items like charcuterie bought over the counter. The reason: Processed meats relied on nitrites as a curing agent and preservative to extend shelf life and ward off premature spoilage or outbreaks of botulism.

Products injected with nitrites — think sodium or potassium salt — cannot be sold as organic or natural, according to the U.S. Department of Agriculture, which oversees the nation's food supply. Instead, such meats are labeled as cured. That distinction had become a turn-off for many consumers who were searching for organic/natural foods and were willing to pay a premium for what they saw as healthier, superior products.

But Bacus had devised a way, employing a particular bacteria as a starter, to use celery as a natural curing agent by converting the plant's high nitrate content into nitrite. He also had figured out a regulatory loophole: The USDA considered celery powder a food in its own right or as a natural flavoring additive — but not as a curing agent.

That meant meat producers could use celery powder not just for flavor, but also as a preservative, and still be able to carry the organic/natural label, once certain other USDA standards were met. And that was a potential game changer because organic and natural products were making major inroads in grocery store aisles and poised to become one of the more coveted sales tags in the food industry.

As Tom Brown put it, "The marketing guys said, 'We love uncured and natural. We want that customer because they pay too much.'"

Bacus concluded he had a winning idea with his starter bacteria, but he needed a partner who could produce a reliable, steady supply of celery powder. He conducted an internet search and discovered Florida Food Products in Eustis, Florida, could fit his needs because of its history with celery concentrate and powder.

Although he did not know it then, Bacus was the third University of Florida affiliated researcher who had contacted the Browns about a new product idea. The previous two had been winners — Ferd LeGrand with turning blemished carrots into juice and Bob Bates recommending the combination of bitter watermelons with a small amount of pesticide to combat corn rootworm beetles in the Great Plains states.

But Bacus had come up with the best idea yet, if the Browns could make it work.

## TURNING CULLS INTO PRODUCT

FFP long had been taking mechanically harvested celery culls — typically tainted by the Blackheart bacteria that made the stalk spotted and unsuitable for fresh sales — and processing them into various products, most prominently a vegetable medley stock, or mirepoix. Duda Farms, based in Oviedo but with major farm lands in South Florida, was one of the main suppliers to FFP.

Teaming up with FFP, Bacus reasoned, made a lot of sense. Bacus, after all, knew all about processed meats and almost nothing about vegetables, while the Browns were in the reverse position of knowing all about vegetables, but very little about processed meats.

So Bacus made the call, got Gator on the phone, told him what he had in mind. About all FFP had to do, he said in so many words, was turn that celery concentrate into powder and mix it with his starter — then, if all went well, watch the money pour in.

Gator was receptive, but puzzled by the concept at first. Why hadn't someone thought of this earlier? Would the USDA really go along with it? He talked with Tom, who was intrigued, but also perplexed. "We got wind of it," Tom said, "but we didn't quite understand it." The more Tom pondered the idea, the more skeptical he became. He figured it was a fad, a passing fancy.

Tom's opinion shifted quickly after Pizza Hut — at Bacus's behest — placed an order with FFP for its high-nitrate celery powder. The Browns then combined their powder with Bacus's enzymes in a brine at meat-processing plants. The brine was injected into the meat that, when cooked, turned the nitrate into a nitrite, curing the food to the red color demanded by consumers. Pizza Hut in turn used the powder on its popular meat toppings like sausage and pepperoni, allowing the chain to sell pizzas that were "natural." To the brothers delight, Pizza Hut promoted their natural pizza in commercials run during the Super Bowl.

The sale gave Bacus's pitch greater resonance with the brothers. "He said this could be big," remembered Gator, who started seriously studying the idea, looking into the USDA regulations, investigating the organic market and estimating potential expenses.

Bacus was so convinced he had a winner that he was ready to quit his job with the Danes and go out on his own, that is, if he had a partner that could provide the celery and, just as importantly, help sell the product to the meat industry. His soon-to-be-former employer was willing to let him use the starter, as long as he bought it solely from the company.

Gator and Tom debated the proposition. On the plus side, the brothers had access to a large supply of celery in South Florida, about 200 miles away, or less than a four-hour drive. The celery could be mechanically harvested and loaded directly into FFP trucks in the field, reducing costs. And FFP was intimately familiar with celery, extracting and drying it for years.

Possible downfalls were the large capital investment, the fermentation process was unpredictable and FFP had little experience with Bacus's bacteria starter. And, even worse, there was no 100 percent guarantee that the USDA would approve — much less that Tom could make a winning sales pitch to the meat packers.

But the pair decided to go all in and bought one dryer, then three more – each one costing $3 million – to ramp up production of the celery powder. That was a major commitment for a company with annual sales of less than $20 million.

## TAKING A CHANCE

Bacus was impressed by the willingness of Gator and Tom to take a chance on him. "They were just crazy enough to go along with it," Bacus recalled. "And one thing led to another."

Gator, meanwhile, instructed his technical staff to start combining the bacteria from Bacus with the celery juice at the FFP plant. 'Sounds easy, but bugs (bacteria) aren't cooperative," he said.

In fact, the bacteria had to be handled just right to avoid contaminating the myriad other products made at FFP. And getting the proper ratios between starter and powder was difficult, particularly when scaling it up to a commercial level and not just as an experimental batch or two.

The celery powder, they learned through trial and error, had to be slowly "cooked" or fermented — at around 98 degrees — with the bacteria starter for its nitrate to be optimally converted to nitrite. An entire day would pass before they knew if they got the batch right. Countless attempts failed.

Without money coming in from existing customers such as the corn farmers and aloe, FFP could not have afforded the experimentation.

In the end, the unsuccessful runs paid off because FFP researchers figured out how to add Bacus's enzyme in Eustis, meaning meat processors only had to add the powder to the meat brine and not expose their plants to the live bacteria being added to the celery powder. That made the product exponentially more attractive to buyers.

As FFP tinkered, the economy was roaring, with the 2007-08 start of the Great Recession still months away. Organic and natural products remained on the upswing, just as Bacus had predicted, going from a nice little niche at Whole Foods to cross over into the major chains such as Publix and Kroger. The products secured prominent displays and space on deli shelves and in coolers across the nation.

That's when Tom Brown and other sales representatives went on the road, calling on meat packers and producers, many of them in the Midwest. It was not necessarily an easy sell. Not only did Tom have to introduce himself, he also had to tell potential clients about a product they may never have considered before. He used Bacus — now a contract employee with FFP — as his technical backup to overcome the initial doubts. "They (customers) needed somebody to hold their hand and walk them through it," Bacus said.

The Browns also hired a recent graduate in Jason Reicks from Iowa State. He was trained in meat formulation and understood the potential of natural and clean label markets. His generation and contacts were populating the research labs, where formulating "natural" meat products was key to building business. Consumers also were switching to clean ingredient listings and preferred celery powder to synthetic sodium nitrites.

But there was unforeseen trouble on the horizon. Just as FFP was making inroads in the market — roughly June of 2006 or 2007 — a large, publicly traded Irish food product company called Kerry Group came out with a patent on fermented celery as a natural meat preservative. Based in Tralee, Ireland, Kerry has 24,000 employees worldwide and annual sales of $7.5 billion during 2018. FFP had anywhere from eighty to ninety workers, depending on the day, and yearly sales that peaked near $70 million under the Browns.

## PATENT CLAIM

Kerry attorneys sent FFP a letter that said the company owned the celery fermentation process, so back off and get out of the business or face us in court. Gator called in a patent attorney, who after some research, admitted there was some risk for the Eustis company. But FFP, the attorney said, most likely could prove "prior art," or, in other words, that they had come up with the idea first, but just had not patented it. That meant they could stay in business and pursue the market.

"Nobody really paid attention to us," Gator said. "We were under the radar."

Legal opinions aside, FFP representatives had to sign documents with just about every account they had saying they would assume liability if Kerry sued. Kerry never followed through and, ironically, the patent dispute apparently kept other competitors from getting into the market. "That was a blessing in disguise," Gator said.

Sales grew slowly but steadily, so much so that FFP became firmly established in the market, even ahead of Kerry. Before long, Tom had deals with major meat producers such as brands including aidells, Boar's Head, Hormel Foods, Jack Link's Beef Jerky, Oberto and Pederson's. "It just kind of took off," said Bacus, who received a commission from FFP on early sales.

"I've got to hand it to them," he continued. "They did a good job."

The Browns work with researchers led to contracts with a host of national meat producers.

Bacus and FFP parted ways in 2011-12, when his technical expertise was no longer critical to the development or sale of the powder and his contract with the company expired. About a year later, the product got a boost when influential professors at Iowa State University gave their nod of approval for celery powder and its role in naturally curing processed meats. Iowa State researchers are well respected in the meat industry.

Joe Sebranek, PhD., Iowa State, in a 2013 video said celery powder was a safe, natural way to cure meat — so effective, in fact, that its use was indistinguishable from artificial nitrites. "They are essentially the same product," he said. "If you put them side by side you'll not be able to tell the difference in terms of color or flavor or anything of that nature."

Bacus agreed, saying that Sebranek was making the same argument he had made for years: That there really is no difference between artificial nitrites or celery powder. The chemical makeup between the two, Bacus said, is the same and the reaction of meat to them produces similar results. "It's all about terminology," he said, referring to it as a "fluke" in the USDA rules.

Fluke or gimmick, Bacus added, celery powder is recognized as legitimate by the USDA and consumers seem to have accepted the concept.

"It was the right thing at the right time."

— JIM BACUS

The key to the entire proposition is an obscure rule in the Code of Federal Regulation called Title 21, Subsection 3. It reads: "Substances obtained by cutting, grinding, drying, pulping, or similar processing of tissues derived from fruit, vegetable, meat, fish, or poultry, e.g., powdered or granulated onions, garlic powder, and celery powder, are commonly understood by consumers to be food rather than flavor and shall be declared by their common or usual name."

The rule also says flavor additives will be considered artificial — thus not natural — if they are not derived from a "spice, fruit or fruit juice, vegetable." It defines a spice as "substances which have been traditionally regarded as food, such as onions, garlic and celery."

At peak, FFP was providing enough powder to cure 500 million pounds of meat a year. They annually were processing 40,000 tons of celery delivered by Duda, enough to represent 13 miles of tractor-trailer trucks parked end to end. That would be on the same roads that Brown Sr., used to line up trucks holding oranges.

The little Eustis plant had corralled roughly 75 percent of the natural, uncured processed meat market. That included items such as hot dogs, sausage, ham, bacon, pepperoni, and deli meats, but not hamburger or chicken — or meat products that are sold fresh.

## ORGANIC MARKET CONTINUES GROWING

FFP's timing with celery powder was close to impeccable. Organic sales of all products have done nothing but climb, even through the recession of 2008-2010. Organics reached a record $49.4 billion in sales during 2017. That's an increase of 6.4 percent, or $3.5 billion, according to the Organic Trade Association's 2018 Organic Industry Survey. The overall food market, by comparison, increased 1.1 percent during the same time period. Organics, the survey said, accounts for 5.5 percent of the food sold on the retail level in the United States. That means there is still plenty of room to grow.

As with other products that FFP sold through the years, Tom said the company prided itself on quality control. FFP did not skimp on getting the formula right or cut corners during the processing, even when it might have been easy to do so and increase profits. Maintaining FFP's good name, Tom said, was paramount from the beginning of his tenure to the end. "Once you give up your reputation, you can't get it back," he said.

Still, Tom is amazed that the USDA does not consider celery powder a preservative. "Fluke of luck," he said.

Gator shakes his head at the success of the celery powder. "It was sweet when it lined up," he said. "It was unbelievable."

# 10

# CRISIS

## LAUNCH FACES COMPETITION, SUPPLY CHALLENGES

Jerry Brown Sr., was an avowed risk taker in business, practically from the day he left the Navy after World War II in 1946 — and certainly from the time he founded Florida Food Products eight years later. "Dad was always throttle down," Gator said. "Dad was push, push, push."

So it was, even two years after he had passed away, that his sons were moving forward on projects he helped set in motion. The problem was the ventures were faltering, essentially all at once, putting the very existence of the company in jeopardy. The year was 1997.

After running the numbers countless times, FFP's chief financial officer (CFO) at the time brought Tom and Gator into his office during the latter part of the year. He showed them a spreadsheet and quietly said, "You all are going to go broke." As if to add an exclamation point to his dire prediction, he quit a week later.

Jim Matteson, who handled the annual tax returns for the business as well as the individual returns for Gator and Tom, said FFP was in an especially bad way financially. "It was pretty bleak," he said, "truly, very bleak."

The crisis was simple to explain, but difficult to solve. The brothers had expanded too quickly during a time of economic uncertainty. "We tried to grow too fast," Gator said. Added Tom, "It was a very critical time for us."

The prime market for two of FFP's most popular and profitable products, aloe and carrots, was Asia. Korea had a strong demand for aloe, while Japan went for carrots. Aloe had provided consistent income for a decade and a half, while carrots had the plant running at full capacity.

But starting in July 1997, much of Asia's economy faltered hard, triggering worries about a worldwide economic meltdown due to financial contagion. The scenario was similar in some ways to the Great Recession of 2007-2010, when the European Union was teetering, thanks in part to the poor financial performance of debt-laden countries such as Greece.

The 1997 crisis started in Thailand, when its currency, the baht, collapsed because the country had borrowed too much money and was falling short on repaying the debt, causing it to approach bankruptcy. Other Southeastern Asian countries saw their currencies fall, too, because they were plagued by the same debt issues.

The International Monetary Fund (IMF) eventually stepped in, spending $40 billion to stabilize the currencies of South Korea, Thailand and Indonesia, the countries that were most severely hit by the economic downfall. The move quelled the international emergency, just as the IMF did nearly two

decades later when it loaned $116 billion to Greece — along
with forcing the country to accept harsh austerity measures.

But the IMF aid in Southeast Asia did little to help FFP
because, in quick succession, the company lost a $2 million-
dollar aloe contract to customer Kim Jong Moon in Korea,
plus another worth nearly $2 million in carrot juice contracts
from Koyo Mercantile of Japan. "They just said, 'No more,'"
Tom recounted.

Carrot sales fell precipitously, too, because of the economic
slowdown and an over-sold market. Other companies had been
getting into carrot production, siphoning off FFP deals.
Making the carrot slump worse was a pending state decision to
buy up muck land on Lake Apopka, which was where FFP
secured most of its carrots. The state spent $200 million
purchasing the farms to stop the pesticide and fertilizer runoff
that was killing the lake and aquatic life by causing massive
algae blooms.

The Browns' and Peters' citrus holdings were miles from
Lake Apopka, but the five farms that sent carrots to FFP were
taken out of production once the state bought the land.

Also hurting FFP was the NAFTA trade agreement the
United States had signed with Canada and Mexico in 1994.
The deal allowed cheaper fruits and vegetables to flow in from
Mexico, undercutting the prices for all facets of the food
ingredient market, including products sold by FFP.

As sales slumped, FFP was stuck with barrels of frozen
carrot juice concentrate and vacuum-sealed bags full of aloe
powder sitting in the Eustis warehouse. The vegetable lines
were processed from January to May because that was when
the crops matured and could be harvested. That meant an

entire year's worth of sales were made during the first five months of the year and were sitting in the warehouse.

## TONS OF PRODUCTS WASTE IN WAREHOUSE

The unwanted stock was worth millions, the demand dramatically reduced because of FFP's constricted marketplace. "When people don't buy it, that's a real problem," Tom said in his typically understated way.

Another financial blow came when the privately held Japanese company San-Ei Gen, based in Sanwa-cho, Toyonaka, Osaka, abruptly pulled out of a partnership with FFP. The two had joined forces several years earlier to produce a red, natural dye derived from a special purple cabbage seed. It was grown in Hastings, Florida, then trucked south to FFP for processing.

San-Ei Gen was represented in the United States by Jeff Greaves, who was based in New York City at the time. Greaves had befriended Tom and approached FFP with the venture, which called for the Japanese to invest up to $10 million in equipment and time in outfitting the plant. Though FFP was not asked to put up any cash, the brothers invested countless company hours.

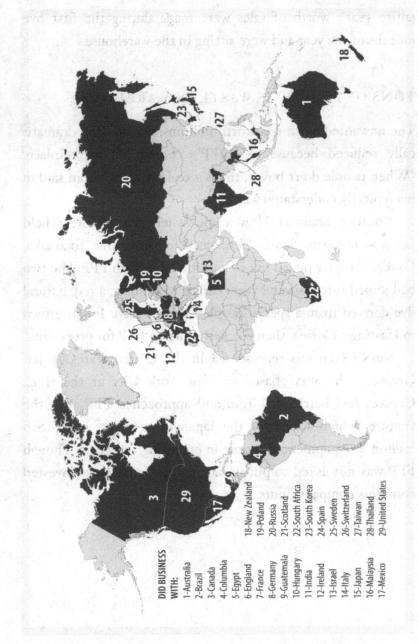

DID BUSINESS
WITH:
1-Australia
2-Brazil
3-Canada
4-Columbia
5-Egypt
6-England
7-France
8-Germany
9-Guatemala
10-Hungary
11-India
12-Ireland
13-Israel
14-Italy
15-Japan
16-Malaysia
17-Mexico
18-New Zealand
19-Poland
20-Russia
21-Scotland
22-South Africa
23-South Korea
24-Spain
25-Sweden
26-Switzerland
27-Taiwan
28-Thailand
29-United States

The idea was to market the product as a natural replacement for Red 40 dye, the most popular coloring formulation on the market. It was used in a variety of products, including foods, drinks and pharmaceuticals — even M&Ms and Pepto-Bismol.

The problem with Red 40 dye, according to the Center for Science in the Public Interest, is it can cause allergic reactions in some people. Red 40 dye also contains p-Cresidine, which the U.S. Department of Health and Human Services maintains can be "reasonably anticipated" to be a human carcinogen.

Adding to FFP's woes was that the spent cabbage, when dispensed on a thirty-acre spray field next to the Eustis plant, gave off a noxious odor reminiscent of sulfur or rotten eggs. Nearby residents complained with a few bumper stickers saying, "What Stinks in Eustis? Florida Food Products." Gator met with them to try and assuage their concerns, but short of ending the arrangement there was little he could do about the stench.

Complicating matters even more, Greaves said, was that San-Ei Gen was led by an "idiosyncratic individual" who inspired fear as much as respect from his employees. "Everyone was afraid to take risks," he said, which he believes led to San-Ei opting out of the deal with little notice.

"We put a lot of time and energy into that project. It hurt," Tom said.

Greaves said he did not know of the financial troubles facing FFP at the time because all he saw was the Brown brothers working hard, as they did day in and day out. "They," he said, "were very good at making a lot out of a little."

## WAREHOUSE EXPANSION SOAKS UP CASH

Another blow, and potentially the fatal one, to the company was an earlier decision to build a 30,000-square-foot warehouse addition in Eustis to store Shasta carbonated beverages. That cost the brothers $1.5 million, but they had used cash reserves for construction, leaving their coffers virtually empty.

So without the normal income from aloe and carrots to meet payroll and other obligations — as the brothers had used in the past — the two had to run through nearly all of a $1 million line of credit. That strategy left the company precariously short on daily operating funds, prompting the CFO to declare FFP was about to go under.

Outside of the value of the property — which was roughly $5 million, according to one appraisal — FFP was bereft of cash at that point. "There wasn't any money," Gator said. "We were broke."

Matteson said, "The issue boiled down to cash flow. Could they survive the (lack of) cash flow at the time?"

Tom took the company's grim plight personally because he was losing accounts he had nurtured since joining FFP in 1983 and moving into sales and marketing. "You work with people for ten years and it's gone," he said.

The brothers longed to talk to their dad and seek his advice. But it was not to be. "We lost our rock," Tom said.

Gator and Tom went to several bankers, seeking another line of credit or a loan, but were rejected because of a lien that had been placed against FFP that they knew nothing about. The claim went all the way back to 1969. That's when Brown Sr., had started losing his canning business following an assembly-line foul up that led to widespread leaks in the beverages his company had sold to soda pop operations in the Caribbean and Puerto Rico.

Brown Sr., had contended the canning equipment was faulty and had stopped paying for it, arguing the breakdown had destroyed his business. The manufacturer countered that people working for Brown Sr., did not operate the machinery correctly and filed a breach of contract lien against FFP. Neither side really pursued the suits in court, causing them to languish for decades.

But after the bankers discovered the dispute, they shied away from loaning to FFP, citing the legal uncertainties. That left the brothers to scramble for funds they did not have. Sleep interrupted by worry became standard for the brothers.

"There was so much stuff going on, we didn't know what to do," said Gator, who despite the financial strain, remained optimistic "I always felt we would pull through," he said. "Maybe I was naive, but I always thought we would make it."

## GATOR SELLS CARROT BUSINESS

In the absence of additional capital, the brothers scrambled to cut costs by laying off several employees and searching the globe for smaller customers to make up for the lost contracts. "Cut costs and sell like hell," Tom summarized.

At the Washington state plant, Tom tried processing wheat and barley grasses into juices to bring in some extra cash, but they did not sell well. He had a bit more luck with turning spinach into a concentrate that could be added to party dips. FFP landed a contract with Sabra for that offering.

"It wasn't easy," Tom said, "but we managed to generate cash flows by discounting inventory and drastically reducing operating costs."

Gator and Tom also decided to sell the carrot business to Bolthouse Farms in California. Bolthouse, which was family owned, was one of the nation's largest carrot growers at the time.

In some ways, it was a good time to sell the carrot operation. The Browns had won a large contract to supply carrot juice to Campbell, which had launched V8 Splash. The carrot-based drink was one of the most successful new product launches in Campbell history. The Browns also knew they would have a hard time replacing much of the carrot supply they were about to lose because the state was purchasing the Lake Apopka muck farms.

"The key is knowing when to get out."

— TOM BROWN

Gator, after three days of hard negotiations with the patriarch of the Boathouse clan, William, sold the Washington state carrot plant they had established three years earlier and all its customer contracts for $4 million, plus 5 percent royalties off the first three years of sales. The total royalty payments ended up exceeding the sales price.

The Bolthouse sale, Matteson said, essentially saved the company. "They were able to re-invent themselves," Matteson said. That adaptability was key, he said, because many family owned companies he has consulted with through the years refuse to change. "A lot of people ride it down to the end," he said.

The Browns also called on an old connection of their father's to bring in some critically needed operating cash to tide the company over until the Bolthouse deal could be consummated.

They went to Tom Johnson, an executive they knew at the First Union Bank office in Eustis. First Union had previously been First Bankers of Orlando, where Brown Sr., once had served as chairman of the board. And First Bankers had absorbed First National Bank of Winter Garden, which had been co-founded by Brown Sr.'s, late father-in-law, Phil C. Peters. First Union eventually was purchased by Wachovia Bank, which was absorbed by the Wells Fargo financial conglomerate.

Johnson, who had known the Browns for years, did some research and decided the lien was close to expired and went ahead and loaned FFP $1.3 million — which was enough to get the company back on solid footing. In the end, Tom said, "1997 was the only year during my tenure at the company that it actually lost money."

Added Gator about the loan: "That was big. Kept us going."

Greaves, who lives in South Florida and runs his own food color and extract business called Food Ingredient Solutions, said the Browns came to his aid in 1999, when FFP was firmly out of financial peril. Greaves, at the time, had been stiffed for more than $450,000 by a company that went out of business, imperiling his operation so much that he feared he would be forced into bankruptcy.

Greaves said he had offers to buy his company at what he considered to be well below market value, but he wanted to keep the business going. The Browns loaned him $90,000, which was enough, he said, to keep the company viable. The Browns eventually agreed to turn the loan into a share of the business, which, Greaves said, was valued at $1 million when they invested but now has annual sales of $25 million. That means the Brown's stake is worth roughly $1 million.

"I like them both," Greaves said. "I consider them my friends. I like them a lot. They are good guys."

# II

## EVAPORATOR POWERS FLORIDA
## FOOD PRODUCTS

### PURCHASE PROVED PRESCIENT

J erry Brown Sr., had one small, single-stage evaporator when he and two partners opened the doors of Florida Food Products in 1954. It was just big enough to compete in the burgeoning orange juice concentrate market, but the company needed more capacity to survive because the competition was growing stronger seemingly by the day.

So, early on, he bought a used evaporator from an Ocala milk-dehydrating plant and melded it with his existing machine to expand it into a three-stage unit, more than doubling its output. That purchase, with the price unknown, created an evaporator still in use today, sixty five years later.

It ended up being one of the most significant moves Brown Sr., ever made.

But instead of turning vast amounts of orange juice into concentrate as Brown Sr., envisioned, the evaporator has been used mostly on a wide range of fruits and vegetables, from aloe

to carrots to beets to watermelons to celery. Those commodities — and not OJ — sustained FFP through the tough times
and eventually made it a thriving business coveted and
purchased not once, but twice, by private equity companies.

Bulky and less inefficient by
today's standards, the evaporator
stands more than three stories
high, at thirty-eight feet, and is
ten feet in diameter, with a stain-
less steel interior and black metal
exterior initially painted blue, the
company's official color. During
the mid-1980s, the brothers had
it painted green to accentuate the
company's move toward natural,
organic products. Brown Sr., had
taken a few days off and was
chagrined to see the change from
green upon his return. "So this is what happens when I leave?"
he asked his sons.

The evaporator combined low heat with vacuum to elimi-
nate water from the juice of fruits and vegetables the company
turned into concentrate. Then, depending on needs of the
client, FFP would contract with nearby driers to make 100
percent juice powders. The evaporator's low temperatures —
typically removing water at 110 to 120 degrees Fahrenheit as
opposed to boiling at 212 degrees — cause less damage to heat-
sensitive enzymes and active plant components, as well as
being gentler on color bodies and flavonoids. Experts say the
moderate temperatures result in a better-tasting product, too.

"It was old, inefficient technology that turned out to be perfect for the emerging dietary supplement and therapeutic juices extracts industry," Tom said.

Though Brown Sr., could not know of the long-range implications of the evaporator and how it would lead to other product lines, he realized pretty quickly that the success or failure of his company was directly linked to the evaporator. If it was filled up and in use, FFP was making money. If it was idle, the money largely stopped coming in. In many ways, it was like a printing press before the internet shook the publishing world. Idle, a press is worthless. But when it runs, it essentially prints money.

At the time Brown Sr., expanded the evaporator, citrus was the sole business for him and his two partners. The evaporator was the key piece of equipment they fired up to concentrate the lower-priced oranges they bought that had been rejected by fresh fruit packinghouses.

The concentrate process called for the fruit to be mechanically squeezed into juice and pasteurized. Then the evaporator took over, transforming the juice into concentrate by removing up to 80 percent of the water. The fruit Brown Sr., trucked in was referred to in the industry as "eliminations" because it was cosmetically flawed, but wholesome otherwise.

When Brown Sr., got to FFP, orange juice had gone from an occasional breakfast drink available seasonally to an immensely popular year-round product, buoyed by the development in 1948 of concentrate. That meant juice could be frozen, shipped all over the world and turned back into a seemingly fresh breakfast drink just by adding three servings of water using the can that held the concentrate.

Touted as one of the healthiest drinks around because of its high vitamin C content, OJ sales grew steadily for years. In 1948, for instance, Florida produced 57.3 million boxes of oranges, according to the U.S. Department of Agriculture. In 1954, that number had jumped to almost 86 million boxes to feed the concentrate craze. Come 1980, when Gator joined FFP, it was a healthy 172.4 million boxes.

But by 2016-17, USDA records indicate, the Florida citrus industry was deep in the throes of a long-term slide, one that might well be impossible to arrest, much less reverse. OJ, because of its high natural sugar content, has fallen into disfavor with many dietitians and health advocates. A series of freezes and a difficult-to-eradicate citrus disease called greening killed hundreds of thousands of orange trees, few of which were replaced. Competition, particularly from Brazil, hurt, too, because the South Americans and other third-world countries rely on cheap labor to grow oranges more inexpensively than their counterparts in Florida.

The most current Florida production numbers, as a result, have fallen to less than 1954 levels, at 68.7 million boxes. In Central Florida — once the hub of the industry — most major groves have been replaced with housing developments, as happened with the property of Brown Sr.'s father-in-law Phil C. Peters in 2005. Outside of the occasional backyard tree and a handful of typically ill-kept small groves, few oranges are grown in Orange County anymore.

But Brown Sr., had no way of knowing in 1954 what the future ultimately held for citrus. His main aim was to make money and provide for his family. Though his means and tools of production might seem primitive now, he often was at the forefront of his industry, maybe not in equipment, but certainly in his approach. Along with his sons, he became a master of taking unwanted fruits and vegetables and squeezing them into profitable commodities.

## RIDING THE POST-WAR BOOM

Brown Sr., started his business in a world that was thriving economically in the aftermath of World War II. Europe and Japan were being rebuilt and hundreds of thousands of ex-servicemen had or were taking advantage of the G.I. bill to earn a college degree, laying the foundation for a thriving American middle class.

Dwight D. Eisenhower was the president from 1953-61, the retired five-star general still popular from his days as the supreme commander of the Allied Forces. He helped spark a huge national investment in infrastructure by getting Congress to agree to build a highway system that would crisscross the country, opening small towns like Orlando and big cities alike to unprecedented growth.

Men were the sole wage earners for most families at the time, which is almost unheard of now. The ties men wore to work were narrow, their suits loose, often grey or muted in color. Wingtip shoes were the fashion. Most women either stayed home with the children or worked in jobs then considered to be appropriate for females, such as secretaries, nurses or teachers.

Close to half of the adult population smoked, compared to one in five now. The Browns were not smokers.

For his part, Brown Sr., left home early for FFP each work

day, often before dawn, as was his lifelong habit — at least until his health faltered badly during the mid-1990s. Back in 1954 when Brown Sr., bought the plant, Caroline stayed home with the children, SuSu, four, and Brenda, two. Jerry Brown Jr. would be born a year later, becoming the first male offspring and earning the nickname Gator after the reptilian mascot of his father's alma mater, the University of Florida.

Gasoline was twenty two cents a gallon then, compared to two dollars now, though the charge fluctuates wildly. A new house cost $10,000, versus the median price of $233,000 now. Driving a Chevy off the showroom floor would cost a little over $1,000. An entry level car goes for at least $13,000 now; a luxury car can easily top $100,000.

Black, rotary dial telephones sat on most office desks during the 1950s, often accompanied by a punch-button adding machine with a side hand crank. Tom remembers that his father kept using such an adding machine until the day he stopped coming into the office because of his failing heart. During their early years with FFP, the brothers used carbon-copy paper and communicated internationally by abbreviated telex because they were charged by the bit.

High-tech back then was the first commercial transistor radio, which was developed by Texas Instruments and went on sale during November, 1954. Calculators would not become commonplace until the 1970s.

## EXPANSION TIMED PERFECTLY

Brown Sr. was so enamored with the evaporator during the early days that he quickly enlarged it, making FFP the tenth biggest processor in Florida. The improvement nearly tripled the evaporator's output, from removing 6,000 pounds of water an hour to 16,000 pounds.

His timing was impeccable because the enhancement occurred just before the 1957 freeze that damaged much of the state's citrus crop, allowing him to buy the soon-to-spoil fruit at discount prices, process them, then sell the concentrate at a premium because he ended up being the quickest to reach a market clamoring for the hard-to-obtain commodity.

He also decided that year to get more into the retail side of OJ by moving from selling in bulk — fifty-five-gallon drums of concentrate — to large companies like Minute Maid and Tropicana and into the 6-, 8- and 24-ounce cans that could be sold under private labels from smaller companies. That necessitated installing new lines that could fill the diminutive cans, rather than the cavernous drums.

The move was a perfect example of one of Brown Sr.'s core beliefs. "'You have to get out of your comfort zone,'" according to Gator. Going in a different or unexpected direction, Brown Sr., believed, could often prove to be profitable, Gator said.

Gator and Tom do not know the company their father bought the composite cardboard cans from, but the lessons he learned from filling them led him to think about getting into the soda business. He knew that carbonated beverages would eat through the cardboard, but he figured a tightly sealed steel can would work. If he was right — and he was — he could run his plant year-round once he started pumping soda into cans. As it stood, FFP was largely idle during the summer, after all the citrus juice was processed.

## SODA POP BECOMES THRIVING CONCERN

Soda was a major gamble because it was only sold in bottles during 1957. Cans, Brown Sr. calculated, were cheaper to produce, stack and transport, plus could be filled faster than bottles. He broached his plan with an old friend, Chapman S. Root, then the largest independent bottler of Coca-Cola in the country. Chapman, whose main office was in Daytona Beach, agreed to the experiment.

Using some of the profits from the recent freeze, Brown Sr. collaborated with other companies to make the cans to hold the soda. He contracted with other firms to rework the filling lines at the plant to accommodate soda during the summer and citrus during the winter, allowing him to keep the Eustis plant running year-round by 1958. That meant he could offer full-time employment, not just seasonal jobs.

Within a couple of years, soda canning had taken off so much that he built seven plants along the Eastern Seaboard and in the Midwest to meet the overwhelming demand. Along with Coke, he also canned for private labels, such as Chek sodas for the Winn-Dixie grocery store chain and Shasta. Initially, he could fill twenty cans a minute, but product demand and efficiency improvements in production upped that number to more than 400. The standard today is more than 2,000 cans a minute. Annual sales for Brown Sr. reached a hefty $15 million in 1967.

The problem for Brown Sr. was the continual production advancements were expensive — too much, in fact, for a small business, especially one as leveraged as FFP, Tom said. Instead of being able to set aside money for upgrades, much of his cash flow went to pay off loans, Gator said.

That's when his father decided to get out of the U.S. soda-filling business. He sold the filling plants to Shasta and Coca Cola, keeping the Eustis complex for citrus. Using the sales cash, he constructed a can-folding plant next to the existing can-filling plant he owned in Puerto Rico.

The canning operation lasted until 1976, though it limped through the last several years after the seals on an immense batch he sold to a variety of customers failed, forcing him to recall the stock and reimburse the cost. He sued the manufacturer of the equipment for selling him faulty machinery, while he was counter-sued for breach of contract. The allegations languished in court for years and never were resolved. The harm to his company's reputation, plus competition from other canners, led him to get out of the business, selling the Puerto Rico plant to the makers of Orange Crush.

By that time, the economy was foundering. Inflation was raging, leading to historically high interest rates. Access to borrowed capital for small businesses like FFP was virtually impossible to obtain and, when it was, the cost was exceedingly high, typically in the double-digit range for interest rates.

Energy costs soared, too, with American production of oil flat, while the Arab nations banded together to form OPEC, a cartel that drove gas prices over a dollar a gallon by the late 1970s. Other forms of energy, such as coal and natural gas, spiked, too. High energy prices cut into Brown Sr.'s operating margins by running up operating costs, from fuel for trucks, to electricity to natural gas to fire up boilers.

## USED TANKS, OLD EQUIPMENT GET NEW LIFE

The evaporator, old, empty tanks and other plant equipment idled by the bad economy and FFP's shallow finances became useful again during the early 1980s, when the company started processing aloe, the cactus-like plant that produces burn-soothing gel and latex substances.

The low-temperature evaporator was ideal for eliminating water from the heat-sensitive aloe gel and turning it into concentrate. The problem was aloe was too expensive to grow in Florida, prompting the Browns to settle on Guatemala to harvest the plant, Gator and Tom said.

They shipped old parts and tanks to the Central American country, but the evaporator could not be moved. So, the Browns pioneered a cold-temperature reverse-osmosis setup in Guatemala, where a semipermeable membrane was used to separate the gel and latex from the water. The aloe inner gel was concentrated ten times then was shipped back to Eustis, where the evaporator finished off the concentration process.

The Eustis plant had freeze dryers by then, too, which were used to turn the concentrate into the industry standard 200-times-strength powder. That level of concentrate was near perfect for cosmetic companies, making FFP one of the leading aloe ingredient suppliers in the country. The brothers sold the Guatemala plant and customer list in 2013 to keep up with the exponentially growing demand for celery powder. "It wasn't so much the money, as the time," Gator said of the decision to sell. "It (aloe) was a management time suck."

That low-temperature evaporator also came in handy when FFP moved into processing carrots during the mid-1980s, which opened up the vegetable concentrate and powder market that would become the signature products of the company during the years ahead. Among them were: beets, onions, bell pepper, celery and watermelon.

The relatively small size of the evaporator was a plus because they were able to experiment with small "boutique" batches of whatever product they were interested in developing, Gator said. If they made a mistake, he said, the losses were kept at a minimum because the batches were not very big.

Gator and Tom also bought a second, more efficient evaporator for $1.3 million in 2012 to keep up with the celery powder production requirements. The brothers spent an additional $400,000 getting it set up in the plant.

At that point, they still were following their father's instinct to keep the evaporators running. From citrus to aloe to carrots to broths to watermelon attractants to celery powder, it was all about "filling up" the evaporator, Tom said.


## FAMILY BUSINESS COMES TO AN END

But it was Brown Sr.'s initial purchase of the old dairy equipment back in 1954 that started it all.

And it was the evaporator, in the end, that made the final sale of Florida Food Products possible — some sixty-two years later, as the remnants of Hurricane Matthew howled onto the property.

Gator was in his office. Tom was at his Winter Park home with his older daughter Taylor. Both brothers were on the phone with the top managers and finance experts from Kainos

Capital, the Dallas private equity firm that intended to buy the company from the Browns.

This was the final walk-through. If everyone said yes, the deal was done, no turning back. A single no could shatter everything.

But one by one, each participant said yes, including Tom and Gator. The call lasted less than fifteen minutes. And that was it. More than six decades of family history had come to an abrupt end for the brothers.

Gator hung up the phone, stared a moment at the white walls of his modest, largely nondescript office, then donned a parka, pulled up the hood and went outside. Immediately pelted by howling winds, his eyes misted and tears fell, mingling with the rain on his face as the finality of the call hit him. "That's it?" he thought. "Money's in the account. Party's over?"

Head down, body bowed against the gusts, Gator made his way about the grounds. He looked, as if for the first time, at the twelve buildings of various sizes and shapes that comprise FFP. The place had been expanded and remodeled continually over the years, yet the original core remained, including one building that dated back to 1946, eight years before his father and business associates bought the property.

"I'm walking around and thinking, 'This isn't mine anymore,'" recalled Gator, who had started for good at FFP in 1980, two years after graduating from the University of Florida. He was sorely conflicted, relieved that the sale had gone through, ending an arduous, emotional two-year process. Yet, he was almost grief stricken. A major link to his father was gone. Though well compensated, his life's calling had ended.

He had been cut adrift. "You can't sell yourself," Gator said of the Kainos transaction. "You're gone."

Conversely, Tom felt little emotionally, even though he, too, had spent his entire professional career at FFP, joining the company in 1983, one year after graduating from Florida State University. "You work, work, work, then you close. It didn't overwhelm me," he said.

A few days later, after Matthew had come ashore in South Carolina and dissipated, the brothers went back to the property. As the sun fell, they sat under a tree and knocked back a couple of shots of *Early Times* whiskey, their father's drink of choice.

"It was terrible," Gator chuckled in describing the *Early Times* taste, though he could have just as easily been talking about the emotional turmoil the sale caused him.

"Seemed anticlimactic," Tom said. "It kind of happens and you move on."

Regardless of the money involved, the deal brought an end to the countless times the Browns walked the grounds of Florida Food Products, talking to and directing employees, making deals and meeting deadlines, changing products, sweating over details large and small, squeezing out profits and being squeezed by competitors and the marketplace. The place they spent innumerable hours working no longer belonged to them, Gator realized as the diminished winds of Matthew bore down on him during the day of the sale.

"Sometimes," Gator said, "I still can't believe it's over."

# EPILOGUE

### RETRACING THE OLD ENSIGN'S STEPS

The weather was cool, windy and wet — fairly common, in other words, for April along the south-west coast of England. Four of the five children of the late Jerry and Caroline Brown had traveled from Central Florida to the small, remote village of Slapton in 2018 to commemorate the seventy-fourth anniversary of the Exercise Tiger tragedy just weeks before the D-Day invasion of Europe during World War II.

Jerry Brown, then a twenty-two-year-old ensign in the U.S. Navy, almost perished during the early morning hours of April 28, 1944, when his ship, the LST 507, was sunk by a German E-boat. In all, 639 soldiers and sailors died during a training run so disastrous that the U.S. government forbade anyone from speaking of it for forty years under penalty of court martial.

While the truth came out when the records were finally declassified in 1984, Brown remained reluctant to talk about what happened, just like the countless veterans of his generation who rarely spoke of their wartime experiences. But based on some of the memories Brown did share with family and friends and written accounts of the event, he acted heroically and undoubtedly saved lives. That includes one soldier who visited Brown years later in Orlando. The visitor thanked the former sailor for giving him his flotation device. The soldier could not swim. Brown believed the decision saved his life, too, because he spent much of his time in the frigid water swimming, keeping warm enough to ward off hypothermia.

Brown, known to his fellow servicemen as Brownie, had alternately bobbed, swum and manned an increasingly crowded raft in the treacherous forty-two-degree waters of the English Channel for hours, as men around him slowly succumbed to the cold. He and more than a hundred others finally were plucked from the sea by the captain of the LST 515. The captain, John Doyle, disobeyed orders to return to port and, instead, returned to the aftermath of the horrific attack. Doyle, as a result, was threatened with a court martial, but was never charged.

"I think about how much it must have made him grow up," Gator said of his father's wartime vicissitudes. "All that death and carnage around him, it's hard to believe."

While at Slapton Sands, Gator and Tom walked across the pebble-strewn beach and put their hands in the sea, confirming it was exceedingly cold. "We didn't have the guts to jump in, much less spend any time in it," Gator said.

Each year, a dwindling number of survivors, their family and friends and Slapton villagers gather on April 28 to remember the sacrifice of the Americans who had trained, lived and died in the South Devon area, near the A379 road between the towns of Kingsbridge and Dartmouth.

Among the hundred or so who attended the 2018 ceremony were Tom Brown, Gator and his wife Lisa, SuSu (Brown) Gordy and her husband Bruce and Brenda (Brown) Holson and her husband Yates Rumbley. The fifth member of the Brown clan, Bill, did not make the trip.

The Browns wanted to honor their father by retracing some of the steps he undoubtedly took during the war. They hoped to sense his spirit by walking the narrow cobble streets, downing a pint in a dark pub, grabbing a handful of wet stones off the beach, tasting the salt in the air.

"I felt like I could see a young kid, excited, never been out of Winter Garden. He must have been so naive," Gator said. "It was an eye-opening experience."

Tom tried to recreate what his father's thoughts might have been all those years ago. "He was on a big hunk of metal," Tom said, referring to his father's ship. "Not a vacation, for sure."

Said SuSu, "We could picture it. Picture the whole thing. We got a real feel for Daddy, what he went through."

The observance was held behind the Slapton Sands beach at a place called Torcross, where a black Sherman tank is mounted on a platform. The rotund, iron-clad vehicle was lost during Exercise Tiger and reclaimed from the Channel floor in 1984, roughly the same time the U.S. Department of Defense released records about the tragedy.

A local minister spoke during the ceremony and two military, color-guard contingents dipped their regimental flags toward the black tank. A wreath was placed on it as well.

"It was a real sweet, small service. Very meaningful," SuSu said.

The Browns were wearing blue ball caps with "LST 507" written on the front and "Ensign Jerry Brown" on the back. Numerous residents of Slapton — population less than 500 — came up to the greater Orlando group, thanking them for the service of Brown Sr.

"We were rock stars there," SuSu said.

The group rented a house in Slapton and dined at a pub lined with old black and white pictures of World War II American soldiers and sailors, some shots showing iconic images of G.I.s sharing candy bars with children. There also were photos of the mass exodus of residents from the area ordered by British authorities because the Allied forces needed room to train. The old village church, for instance, became an officers headquarters.

## EXERCISE TIGER FIASCO

The Americans and British trained in the area because it was akin to the Normandy coast of France, where Operation Overlord would take place on D-Day, June 6, 1944. Slapton's rocky beach and sloping, even mountainous, terrain was similar in many ways to the Utah Beach landing area of Normandy, which the group was assigned to invade. There also was a natural slough between the beach and the mainland. At Utah Beach, the Germans had flooded land between the beach and land to slow down possible invaders.

Exercise Tiger was designed to mimic what the Allies would experience on D-Day. The convoy, loaded fully with soldiers and equipment, was supposed to go out into the Channel, then return to the beach to simulate a landing. Live ammunition was supposed to be shot over their heads, giving them an understanding of the horrendous noise and confusion they would face.

But the maneuvers were calamitously interrupted when four German E-boats on patrol happened upon the convoy and attacked. Two LSTs, including the one carrying Brown Sr., were sunk by E-boat torpedoes, while a third was hit, but managed to return to port. The E-boats escaped untouched.

Worried about morale and possibly tipping their invasion plans to the enemy, British and American authorities told all the survivors they were never to speak of what happened. Basically, they were given a few days off to recover, then it was back to the war. Brown was reassigned to a ship that swept Utah Beach for mines on D-Day.

Seventy-four years later, the residents of Slapton have not forgotten the loss of American life and they repeatedly thanked the Browns for the sacrifices made by their father and many of his unlucky mates.

While dining at the Slapton pub, SuSu said, a man came up to them and gave them a spent shell casing from a Remington rifle and a metal piece of shrapnel from the beach, which does not have sand, but rather smooth pebbles ranging in size from a quarter inch to several inches.

Brenda loved the experience: "It was really touching. Everyone, it felt like, knew we were there. I would go back there in a skinny minute."

After Slapton, they ferried across the Channel and toured the Normandy beaches, where a few German concrete bunkers and pill boxes remain imbedded on the hillsides. A memorial plaque at Utah Beach lists all the ships that took part in the invasion, including the Staff, on which Brown Sr., served. The LST 507, lost during Exercise Tiger, is not mentioned.

They also visited the nearby American cemetery in Colleville-sur-Mer. More than 9,000 Americans who died in World Wars I and II are buried there, including two sons of President Teddy Roosevelt.

One night, the group dined in a restaurant in St. Mere Eglise, where paratroopers were slaughtered by Germans while drifting down from their planes during the pre-dawn hours of D-Day. They had overshot their landing zone, leaving them defenseless to the enemy on the ground. The Germans pointed floodlights skyward to illuminate their prey.

The Browns also stayed several nights at a hotel overlooking the La Fiere Stone Bridge, where a fierce battle took place between American paratroopers and German soldiers. The Americans prevailed, securing the main crossing over the Merderet River for miles in either direction.

While at dinner, the Browns signed their names to a board filled with those of other veterans and their families. Some 20 villagers clapped as the Browns wrote their father's name along with LST 507.

## FAMILY DONATES TO MEMORIAL

The family was so moved by the experience that they gave $25,000 to the Exercise Tiger Memorial site in Slapton. The money came from an inheritance of nearly $1 million from their parents that the siblings decided to place with the

Central Florida Foundation, an Orlando nonprofit that manages donation funds and advises philanthropists.

The Exercise Tiger contribution elicited an enthusiastic reply from Dean Small, the Slapton volunteer who tends to the tank and the annual ceremonies surrounding it. He took over the duties after his father, Ken, died.

"This is so wonderful," he wrote the Browns. "For the first time since my dad (Ken) passed away (2004) I can now make the improvements to the Exercise Tiger Memorial where Laurie, Sarah and I met you all! What a great time we had.

Sarah & I still talk about that meeting, in a great way! From us all, THANK YOU!! When I am over the shock I will write something that makes sense but in the mean time, thank you so, so much."

Gator wrote back on behalf of the family: "Truly our pleasure. It is us who should be thanking each of you for your dedication and perseverance for maintaining this enduring monument and honoring so many souls."

The Browns also have used the Foundation to donate $70,000 to the community theater in downtown Winter Garden. Among other possibilities, they are contemplating giving to a drive to build a new branch of the YMCA in Eustis.

Gator, who has been known to pay for the groceries of strangers in line behind him at a supermarket, said he feels an obligation to share his good financial status with others who are less fortunate.

"Lisa always says, 'What goes around, comes around.' You know, karma. I didn't always believe that, but I do now," Gator said.

Brown Sr. and his wife Caroline were not institutional donors, preferring to make contributions on a more personal basis. Brown Sr., for example, often paid for a cabin for underprivileged youngsters at Camp Wewa, a rustic YMCA retreat north of Lake Apopka. "When he made money, he gave money," Tom said.

The funds the Browns left their children, however, turned them into much larger benefactors posthumously. "I think they would be very proud of what we did," Gator said. "They'd like it."

Gator said one way his father gave back to the community

was by introducing young boys to nature. For years, he set up an annual deer and raccoon hunt for friends, employees and their sons at a country lodge he built on property he leased in the Ocala National Forest, north of Eustis.

During a long weekend each fall, the boys would sit in elevated stands with their fathers, waiting for deer to run by after being roused by hunting dogs. At night, they would look for raccoons.

In the end, the boys and their fathers essentially spent quality time together. Gator cannot recall anyone ever actually shooting and killing a deer or raccoon.

Monty Gatch, whose father worked with Brown Sr. for years, fondly recalled the outings. "There was nothing they (the senior Gatch and Brown) wouldn't do for us kids," Monty said.

The Browns also hunted quail, turkey and deer on some 10,000 wilderness acres that were turned into the massive Hunter's Creek residential development in south Orange and north Osceola counties. Along with several other families, the Browns leased and managed the land, as well as hunted on it, with a crude cabin built on stilts near Shingle Creek as the base camp.

"All the Brown boys hunted and spent the night there through our teen years," Tom said.

They typically spent much of their summers on the house on the west side of pristine Lake Butler in west Orange. The summer place was originally owned by Phil C. Peters, but he lost it during some down years in citrus. Brown Sr., bought it back in 1960.

"Growing up, we spent the month of August every year

boating, skiing, swimming generally shoeless," Tom said. "The Summerport house was Mom's and Dad's happy place."

Brown Sr. also hosted a dove shoot every year in west Orange County, along Phil C. Peters Road, named after his late father-in-law. The event typically drew one hundred or more men and youngsters, Gator said.

"Anybody who hunted wanted to come," Gator said.

One year, it was mistakenly shut down by a state wildlife official because he wrongly believed that Brown Sr. had not followed the rules for attracting dove to the field where the shoot was to take place. The official not only forbade the hunt, but he handed out tickets to many of the participants.

Former FFP vice president Charlie Hamrick said Brown Sr. was so upset by the cancellation that he smashed his shotgun through the front windshield of his truck. "He was not happy," Hamrick said.

Brown Sr., drove to Tallahassee the following Monday to complain to wildlife officials. They rescinded the tickets and admitted they were in error, Gator said, but would not apologize in writing.

## REMEMBERING LOYAL EMPLOYEES

When Tom and Gator were negotiating the sale of the family business, they decided that they wanted to share their financial gain with a dozen long-serving employees at FFP — their jobs ranging from hourly floor workers to upper management.

A total of $3 million in bonuses was paid out to them when the private equity firm Kainos Capital resold the company.

The transaction to another private equity firm was finalized during the summer of 2018.

One of those who received a check was Hank Bodden, 58, who was with FFP for twenty-six years. The bonuses — and the individual amounts — were not publicly disclosed. Bodden started out as a temporary employee who did everything from driving forklifts to running the blending and packaging machines.

Bodden, now the blending-room manager, said he has deep respect for the Brown brothers. "They owned the place," Bodden said. "But they were here every day. They were dedicated."

The Browns even hired Bodden's oldest son, Miles, to work at FFP. He left in 2013, after spending eight years at the plant.

Bodden was with FFP through good times and bad, including the lean late-1990s, when the business nearly failed. He knew sales were down, but he had no idea how close to closing up shop they were. "I always got paid. I guess that's why I never thought it was as bad as it was," Bodden said.

## FATHER'S INFLUENCE STILL RESONATES

Though he died in 1995, Brown Sr. still remains a presence in the lives of his children. The decisions he made, the life he led, continue to exert a strong influence in the people they have become and the way they conduct themselves.

He did not offer unsolicited advice, typically venturing an opinion only when he was asked. But based on his lifelong pursuit of entrepreneurship, it is hardly a surprise that all five of his children were self employed, following in their father's well-trodden path.

Brenda, for example, came back to Central Florida in 1985 after graduating from the Vanderbilt University School of Medicine and finishing her residency as a pediatrician in Chicago. At first, she considered signing on with an established Orlando practice.

"Why join a practice when you can build a practice?" Brown Sr. asked Brenda.

She thought about his words, then took the leap, setting up shop with another doctor at their newly christened Casselberry Pediatrics, near State Road 436 and Lake Howell Road. Seminole County at the time had few pediatricians and, as an Orlando bedroom community, was about to explode with young, chid-bearing families.

"He was absolutely right, of course," Brenda said. "We grew like crazy."

Brenda eventually ran the largest pediatric practice in Metro Orlando with ten pediatricians and four nurse practitioners. Her first patients, though, were her son and her partner's children.

Now retired, Brenda travels often with her husband. She has one son, Rush Holson, who lives in Chicago and runs a subsidiary of a business his father's family operates, Guaranty Trust Life in Glenview Illinois. Rush is married to Nicolle and they have two children, Finn and JoJo.

SuSu, the first-born of Jerry and Caroline Brown, was married in 1975 to Bruce Gordy. They met at Mercer University in Georgia, where she was a cheerleader and Gordy was a

basketball player. He became a dentist after graduating from
the Medical College of Georgia.

Brown Sr. had the same advice for the young couple as he
did for Brenda. Go out on your own, he told Gordy, don't work
for someone else. Gordy set up shop in College Park, a neighborhood just north of downtown Orlando teeming with young
families.

Gordy has successfully practiced in College Park for more
than forty years and, starting in 2017, shares his practice with
his daughter Caroline. She graduated from Vanderbilt University with a degree in engineering, then went on to graduate
from New York University's College of Dentistry.

The Gordys have four children. Chance is a senior vice
president of Inverlad Development LLC in Orlando. He is
married to Gina, who has a son, Quinn, from a previous
marriage. Caroline McHugh has two children, Maggie and
Nelle. Hunter is a vice president of national accounts for
Nephron Pharmaceutical in West Columbia, South Carolina.
He is married to Amy Witherspoon and they have two boys,
Hunt and Grant. Maggie Gordy lives in Bozeman, Montana,
and is a territory manager for the pharmaceutical company
Allergan.

Bill, who is married to the former Chris Holt, lives in
Tampa, where he is a real estate developer. They do not have
children. A high school quarterback like his father, Bill is a
former chairman of the Tampa Bay Port Authority

## FAMILY BUSINESS KEPT GATOR, TOM CLOSE TO THEIR FATHER

Tom and Gator stayed close to their father by working for and with him for a decade and a half at Florida Food Products. Gator, in fact, owes his marriage to Brown Sr.

The former Lisa Goodrum made a cold call at Florida Food Products in 1982. She was selling telephone products and had arranged an appointment with Brown Sr. He took a liking to her, so much so that he told her that his oldest son Gator was in charge of such decisions. Lisa did not know it, but Brown Sr. was more interested in her meeting Gator than in the equipment she was selling.

Lisa had no idea of Brown Sr.'s true intent. "I was all prim and proper," Lisa said of meeting Brown Sr. and then Gator for the first time. "Gator was all cocky. Typical Gator."

Gator recommended discussing her proposal over lunch and suggested that they go to the Lamp Post restaurant in Mount Dora, now closed, but a popular spot then. Gator asked that she pay for the meal. "He said, 'You have the big expense account,' which I didn't. I was broke," said Lisa, who picked up the check nonetheless.

Lisa did not close the phone deal with Gator, but they did decide to meet again for drinks. "At that point," Lisa said, "it was definitely more than just business."

Gator eventually purchased some telephones, but Lisa had switched accounts by then and was not credited with the sale.

The pair dated for two years and were married in 1984. At the wedding reception — held at the Mount Dora Yacht Club

— Brown proudly reminded everyone that he was responsible for the two getting together.

"I loved his (Gator's) dad," Lisa said. "He was firm, he was generous. He was a gentleman. He always looked out for other people. He was loyal."

Gator credits Lisa with much of the success the brothers had with FFP. She often counseled him, he said, to be patient or understanding when he would come home frustrated with the work of an employee or a foul-up at the plant.

She frequently handled his business travel arrangements as well as setting up reservations for dinner or lunch with contractors or clients.

More importantly, Gator said, she kept the family bonds strong when he was distracted by work or on the road.

"She maintained the family values," he said, "the core values."

Lisa and Gator have three children: Alexander Z, who goes by AZ, and is named after his grandfather. He has a master's degree in finance from Wharton College and is co-operator of a private equity fund based in New York City called North Current Partners. Audrey, who graduated from Auburn University, is married to Brad Goodwin, a Tampa healthcare marketing consultant with Accenture. They have two girls, Lila and Molly. Nelson, whose name is an homage to a close friend of Brown Sr., real estate investor Nelson Boice, followed his grandfather to the sea and is a lieutenant in the U.S. Coast Guard, based in Charleston, South Carolina. He graduated from the U.S. Coast Guard Academy in New London, Connecticut.

Tom said the most important gift his father gave him was

time together. For several years during the late 1980s, Tom, Gator and their dad shared a small office, all three of them jammed behind their desks. Brown Sr., Tom said, would spend about four hours a day with them, typically during the middle of the week. They would go to lunch together and discuss strategy.

"He never really told me what to do. He let me make mistakes, understand the pain of it. As a parent myself, I appreciate letting kids learn on their own," said Tom, who added that his father often spoke of dealing honestly and ethically with customers.

Tom has two daughters, Taylor and Casey, with Barbara Brophy Brown. Taylor is working in outdoor adventures in Telluride, Colorado, while Casey, the youngest Brown of her generation, is pursuing a master's degree in business.

## THE BROWN BROTHERS BECOME INVESTORS

After selling Florida Food Products, Tom and Gator formed a new company, JTB Horizons. Funded in part with proceeds from the FFP sale, they invest in small operations in need of loans ranging from $1 million to $5 million.

So far, they've made six deals, working with companies specializing in real estate, farm services and pharmaceuticals. Gator's son, AZ, often reviews the propositions, using his financial expertise from Wharton and previous experience with other financial firms.

Tom looks on the new venture with his brother as a form of good will. "The most philanthropic thing you can do," Tom said, "is create a job."

Gator (left) and Tom Brown at the College Park Cafe, circa 2020. The diner is less than two miles from the office where their father, Jerry Brown, ran the company the brothers took over and turned into a food ingredients juggernaut.

CPSIA information can be obtained
at www.ICGtesting.com
Printed in the USA
LVHW040137030720
659565LV00004B/147